HIGH ENERGY PURPOSE

How To Be All In On Your Life And Find Your Truth

BY JOE APFELBAUM

DEDICATION

To all the souls that are in search of a better life.

To all those who are hungry looking for meaning and purpose.

To all my mentors, coaches and teachers that have guided me in life.

TABLE OF CONTENTS

PROLOGUE

I used to think that I was an idiot, a loser and that no one could possibly love me.

Whaaaat? How could I think something like that?

Let me explain...

When I was 9, I got up to read something in class and I was struggling.

I remember the entire class was laughing at how difficult it was for me to read and the shame of looking like a fool destroyed me.

The memory of being yelled at by my teacher and him shouting: "sit down and shut up you idiot!" while everyone laughed is raw.

I was crushed.

After that incident, I decided never to get up again and be that fool that everyone laughs at and for the next 12 months I came to school late every day and cried.

As I recall these memories, I feel the lump in my throat and my chest tightening up.

Even as a 42 year old, I cry when I think about that poor 9 year old that believed the words of his teacher that were seared in his mind forever.

"I am an idiot"

"I will never speak in public."

"I will never be successful."

"I will never have friends."

"I am not worthy of love and acceptance."

"I am a loser."

In 4th grade, I decided that I was going to rebel. I wanted to prove my teachers wrong.

I decided to go give the system the finger and fight back.

I did that by memorizing everything my teacher said and I sat in the front of the class and I got the teacher to love me.

I was the first to pick up everything and I got 100 on all the tests with my inability to read properly and everything.

I wanted to win over my classmates too so I started making jokes and I got the entire class to laugh constantly.

This became my MO.

Smart kid, top of the class but disrupts everything in class and the teacher has no choice but to kick him out.

Sure, they had to make me valedictorian but they didn't want me in the classroom because I somehow took control away from the teachers with my wit and my pranks.

My parents sent me to Montreal because I was kicked out of the schools in New York.

That only lasted 9 months so the next year they sent me to South Africa I got kicked out too after 6 months.

They sent me to Israel...

I got to travel the world as a brilliant clown who knew the material but had zero discipline.

The rabbis gave me my diploma and ordained me as a Rabbi but didn't want me around because I didn't take life seriously, I was too free-spirited and had too much fun.

When I entered the business world, I found my home.

A place where if you didn't have discipline, no matter how smart you were, you would not succeed.

That was a challenge for a raging idiot who could not read.

I took on the challenge to build a business and built one of the fastest-growing companies in the US and finally, I made it!

But the voice inside me got louder. I could not hear anything other than

"You are an idiot"

It was not until I did the deep work to look inside that I was able to see that this voice WAS NOT ME!

There are so many people who made it to the top of the ladder of success and realized when they got all the way to the top that the ladder was leaning against the wrong wall.

Success and fulfillment are not the same things.

When I interview leaders of the fastest growing companies in the US, they often confess that while they have lots of money, they sometimes feel like they lack purpose.

What is Purpose? How does one find it?

I remember looking around at my life and thinking to myself, I bought the house, the car, the vacation home, I have the kids, the wife, and everything is perfect but something feels off.

I was overweight, my relationship was dysfunctional, I was hungry for more but what was it? Why was I obsessed with personal development?

After working with dozens of coaches, reading hundreds of books and taking many 50 hour workshops I discovered something that no one can show you.

Purpose is not something that you FIND, or that you are GIVEN.

It cannot even be explained or taught.

Purpose is something you need to become aware of. That awareness does not happen overnight.

Once you see it and experience Purpose, you cannot unsee it.

Hopefully this book will help you find your purpose the way the ideas helped me find mine.

When you find your purpose both internally and externally you only have to remain aware and no matter what happens in your life, you can keep moving forward.

It's the foundation for progress, success and fulfillment.

If you want to have more power, more freedom and more vitality, lean into these ideas and let's explore purpose together.

As I rewrite this book, I went through many changes and transformations, a difficult divorce, lost business partners, almost lost my businesses during a global pandemic but I held on strong and I keep moving forward because I am committed to taking action.

Taking actions everyday, no matter what happens, I believe that all things happen in our favor. As long as you can see that and accept it, you can keep moving forward.

WHO THIS NETWORKING BOOK IS FOR

This book is for people who want more out of life.

People who know that there is more to life, rather than just going after their desires.

If you are tired of half-assing your way in life and want to be all in, read this book and you will experience something powerful.

They say the truth will set you free. You are the truth. Your experience is your truth and you are your experience.

Create a more empowering truth by focusing on your purpose, instead of thinking that you are not enough.

Once you discover who you really are and what your internal purpose is, and you align it with your external purpose, you will have the clarity you need to consistently take massive action.

Want results in your life?

Read this book and take some notes.

Share it with a friend, internalize it and you will become a more empowered being. Boom!

Joe Apfelbaum - Author

Feel free to reach out to me at joe@joeapfelbaum.com with the insights you got from this book and how you will be applying them to your life.

If you want to tell your friends about this book, take a photo of yourself with the book cover and post it on social media, use hashtag #highenergypurpose so I can find your posts and give them some love.

Let's get started with the first step: Awareness.

"The first step towards change is awareness. The second step is acceptance." **Nathaniel Branden - Author of the Six Pillars of Self Esteem**

CHAPTER ONE: ACCEPTANCE

WHAT IS AWARENESS?

Awareness is the ability to observe your thoughts, your words, and your feelings; the knowledge that if you can observe a thought, that you are not the thought.

The conscious ability to observe the voice in your head that is constantly analyzing, labeling and subtitling the world for you.

"You might say, what voice in my head?"

That is the voice I am talking about, The one that does not let you stop thinking.

We are always thinking, evaluating and wondering. We are measuring, qualifying and quantifying. Dreaming, desiring, thinking and speaking.

Some people have the voice in their head on speakerphone and everyone can hear everything they are thinking.

We call those people crazy.

But honestly, we are just as crazy, except for the fact that it's a secret.

Only we know how crazy we are to judge everything, label everything and stress about the things that we cannot control.

That awareness itself is known as consciousness. We cannot understand consciousness, we can only experience it. Even labeling it as awareness or consciousness is limiting that experience.

* * *

When you enter a forest and you stop thinking about the trees and all the complexity, and you just take it all in with your 5 senses, you are experiencing.

The one who experiences those things is not the same as the experience itself.

How do you know that you are not a glass of water? Because you can experience the glass of water. You can see it, hold it, smell it, taste it etc. same with your thoughts. If you can experience your thoughts, you are not your thoughts.

If you can experience your feelings, you are not your feelings.

We often confuse our feelings with WHO we are.

"I am angry," or "I am happy" - No. You are only angry if you are not aware, that it is not you that is angry.

You are just experiencing anger and you are observing the feeling.

When you get lost in your feelings, thoughts and actions, you end up losing your awareness and you become that feeling.

You become that thought. You become that action.

For you to have awareness and for you to remain conscious, you must not allow yourself to get lost and forget that you are the observer.

The observer has more power when the observer is aware that it is just a passenger and not the CAR.

The observer has more choice when it realizes that it is not the ANGER, but it is experiencing anger, due to some thought, story, or event that happened.

When you detach yourself from what happened, that is when you have awareness.

You have the ability to observe your thoughts, without thinking that you ARE your thoughts. It's not easy. It takes practice.

We get lost in our thoughts and we forget that we are observing them. We become our thoughts and we get worried, stressed, bored, angry, frustrated and happy.

When our thoughts become feelings, we have a greater opportunity to wake up.

The reason I wrote this book is to wake you up and remind you of WHO you are. You cannot be at 100%, and living a life of purpose, if you have no idea who you really are.

Once you have awareness, only then can you begin to discover a new world of possibilities that you never thought was possible because your thoughts are not you.

This might be a lot to take in and most people that never heard of this concept will reject it instantly. This is normal because you do not want to feel out of control.

We can only control what we understand, but awareness is not something that you can understand. It's something that you must experience.

Being conscious is an experience. It's being alive.

The biggest regret people have is getting to the end of their life, and realizing that they never really lived.

They realize only then, that they do not have the freedom to choose what thoughts to detach from, or what feelings to avoid reacting to.

Life becomes a lot less stressful when you are able to stay in your seat of awareness.
Staying in that seat of awareness takes practice.

It can be as simple as focusing on your breathing and experiencing each inhale and exhale, as it happens with the automatic intelligence that your body has built into it.

Staying in your seat of awareness is a beautiful place to be.

For those who experience it, they want to be there more often, as it connects you with everything in the universe.

We are human beings. That means that we are meant to BE.

We often forget that and we confuse being with doing. That is where stress comes in.

***

Have you ever gone to a movie and watched the movie with so much intent you forgot you were watching the movie and just got pulled into the movie?

That happens to me all the time. I watch an amazing movie and two hours flash by.

Life is like a movie. You have the ability to observe life and remain aware that it's all just a movie or you can forget that life is a movie and you start getting angry about what is going on in the movie because you believe you are IN THE MOVIE.

Remember that you cannot change what happens in a movie. You can only change which movie you decide to watch.

If you do not like your life, remember that you can watch another movie.

You can only do that if you are the observer of life instead of being the actor in life.

Learn to observe while you participate. It's a challenge for most people but it's a skill you can learn. As you keep reading you will learn why it's so important to be an observer if you want to live your purpose.

High Energy Observation: Notice the voice in your head and write down what it's saying to you right now about this chapter. You cannot see the thoughts unless you write them down and read them so take a moment and jot down some notes now.

HOW TO STOP SUFFERING IN LIFE

We all experience suffering in life. We feel pain that we do not want to feel.

Something happened and we want to change what happened. We try to change it with our thoughts, but we fail.

We wish it never happened. And the more we try to change the past, the more we suffer.

We are worried about the future and we feel tortured because we feel like it is going to get worse.

We read the news and see all the reports of current events, and we start to suffer.

We remember the parts of our life that makes us feel guilt, shame, or loneliness, and we want it to change.

Suffering is wanting something to be different, and not having the ability to make it be different.

It could be something simple like being bored and not wanting to be bored. Often it's being tired and not wanting to be tired.

Maybe it's something deeper. Like feeling broke and not being able to buy basic necessities for ourselves or for our family.

We break down, we cry, and we suffer. We pray that somehow things will change in our life.

That somehow, things will be better in the future than they are right now. But deep down inside we do not believe it.

We feel hopeless, but we know we do not want to feel that way. So how do you stop the stress?

How do we get out of the mess?

We can analyze this all we want, but it will not get us very far because we will get stuck in the paralysis of analysis.

What creates the stress is our thoughts themselves. And the lack of oxygen that follows when we hold our breath.

Instead, we need to detach ourselves from the thoughts and feelings, and observe them without labeling them, without judging and just be with them.

All thoughts and feelings are fleeting, which is to say that they come and go.

I want you to say out loud, "This too shall pass." Now, take a deep breath in from your nose, fill your belly and out from your mouth.

High Energy Observation: Write down the things you worry about that you cannot change and ask yourself if it's worth your time and effort to worry about these things, especially knowing the fact that there's nothing you can do about it.

THE EGO DOES NOT WANT US TO BE AWARE

"Wait a minute. Are you telling me that I have an EGO?" Did your ego just get insulted by getting observed by your awareness? YES!

The EGO is darkness and your awareness is light.

What happens when you turn on a DROP of light in a huge amount of darkness?
The darkness just disappears instantly.

EGO disappears effortlessly, just like darkness disappears in the face of light.

Our EGO will try to hold on to the darkness, (that is the lack of awareness), for as long as possible.It will confuse it with your very survival.

When someone YELLS at me or disrespects me, I feel like I MUST RESPOND right away. I must defend my honor.

If I do not defend myself and I just take it, I feel like I will die.

What is happening there is, the EGO is trying to protect itself the way it does that is by making me feel like if I do not respond, it will get worse, I will suffer and eventually die.

* * *

So I react without thinking and I get angry and I justify my actions and the EGO gets bigger because I YELLED back,

16

because I put the other EGO in check and defended my honor.

Sometimes that EGO will use other peoples honor as the justification to react.

The key is to become aware that every role we have in life right now is part of our EGO and when we attach ourselves to those roles, we become those roles.

I am a father, and when my child is disrespectful, my EGO gets angry. If I am in my seat of consciousness, I might still discipline my child for being disrespectful, but I will not lose myself and get angry.

I will not hit my child and feel justified. Instead I will find ways to educate and inspire my child with love. Discipline my child with respect and dignity.

Any role that I have in my life can be enhanced with awareness and consciousness, because it will allow me to choose my response to the environment as I fulfill my obligations in that role.

We often confuse our role with WHO we are and that allows our EGO to take over and we are no longer aware.

To be enlightened means to remain aware, alive and present when you live your life.

But what happens when we want to change something in our life that DOES not want to change?

Like our spouse, we want to change our partner!

Our partner is not growing or they are growing out of control.

Realize that you cannot change what is not you.

High Energy Observation: Think about the things that you are affected by? How much your life is being affected by external circumstances? Can you be aware and observe this as the EGO? Do not notice how the EGO does not want you to see this part of yourself?

WHY RESISTANCE LEADS TO PERSISTENCE

I never understood that I cannot change what is not me. I believed that I can change things in my life, I can change people. I can change jobs, roles, locations.

The more things change, the more they stay the same.

I recently had a conversation with a man who was in his 4th marriage and I asked him how this most recent marriage was going.

He confessed that he kept trying to change wives and hoped that his problems would improve in his relationship.

He said they are all the same.

I asked him what they all had in common.

He said he wishes he knew.

Well, he didn't know because he was not aware.

He is the common denominator to all his problems and you are the common denominator to all your problems.

You cannot fix a problem with the same logic that created the problem in the first place.

You need transformation not change. Change is more of the same, it's bringing the past into the present and then into the future.

If you want a different future, you need to transform the NOW which is a foundation for what is coming next.

Remember that your past does not need to equal your future, unless you lack awareness and you keep resisting your NOW.

The first step to awareness is acceptance that where you are RIGHT NOW is EXACTLY where you need to be.

If you cannot change what is NOW, BE with what is now.

When you accept, your energy becomes more peaceful and you can allow the transformation process to begin.

As long as you KEEP PUSHING, you will get more resistance. The best way to win an argument is not to argue.

The best way to stop a fight is to take the power and energy away, by unplugging. No more responding, no more giving away your power.

But you might be thinking, that is not FAIR.

I want to win! I need to show them. I need to be RIGHT. A coach once told me, "You can be right or you can be happy."

What he didn't tell me is that I need to be in my seat of awareness to really choose because my EGO always wants to be right.

My EGO wants to get bigger, wants to WIN more, wants to expand.

There are times where expansion is important but there are times when the WAVE needs to return to the ocean. The EGO wants to flood the town so it just keeps growing and causes a tsunami. People get hurt in your raging storm.

When you accept that you are but a wave, you surrender to the ocean and you enjoy the wave while it's growing, but you also learn to enjoy the wave while it's going back to its source.

* * *

The famous saying is; "You are either growing or dying." Your EGO always wants to be growing and expanding.

The EGO will naturally find a way to feed itself by changing everyone else around you, and protecting itself from anything that will question its motives.

The EGO can only exist in thought. If you stop thinking the EGO goes away.

High Energy Observation: Resisting something that you cannot change leads to more resistance which leads to more disappointment. Write down the things that you are resisting in your life right now. Can you change it? Then take action. If not, then just let it be and accept the things you cannot change.

THINKING CREATES REASONS NOT PURPOSE

When you are so busy thinking you stop living. You are now in your head. If you are in your head you are dead. Want more peace? Be with what is in the now.

When we try to think and solve problems, we usually come up with lots of excuses, reasons why things are the way they are. Reasons why it's not our fault and if only things were different.

These reasons are excuses and you either have reasons or you have results.

You can make all the excuses you want in the world, but realize that the only reason you need reasons and excuses is to justify something.

Be unreasonable and take action that is above reason.

Not responding to your EGO, even if you feel like you are dying inside, is being unreasonable.

You have every reason in the world why you are justified to feed into the BS that is being fed to you, but you need to breathe deep and let go.

Accept and this wave of energy will pass, instead of swallowing you up.

* * *

Thinking will give you reasons not to transform.

"If it ain't broke, don't fix it." That's what they say. "Why try to shake up the tree, live and let live."

But you are feeling frustrated, annoyed, out of your element. How do you find that peace again? Why does your mind make you crazy?

Your EGO is making you search for something that does not exist.

It's kind of dysfunctional in a way. Because what we really want is to experience joy, freedom, peace, love, and creativity, but our EGO makes us believe that control is more important.

Accept that there is a greater intelligence than your own thinking that you are tapped into.
Your body works to keep you alive and thriving without your thinking.

Allow your spirit to tap into the same intelligence and start flowing.

Stop being so clever and trying to get rich quick, lose weight fast, but instead realize that slow and steady wins the race.

What is it about us that we want to be so clever?

High Energy Observation: Can you notice moments when you were so immersed in thought that you tuned out the current moment? Are you scanning and searching and trying to fix things? Just notice those moments that you are not present and catch yourself. Take a deep breath and just notice. The faster you catch yourself, the better you become at noticing.

STOP BEING SO CLEVER

A fox is sly, it likes to make tricks and win over its friends. Your mind is pretty clever too. Our EGO uses you to win over people, to force them to like you.

This is not always the most intelligent way to be. Always having an agenda, always trying to win every battle.

Often we win the battle because we are so clever but we lose the war because we are not being intelligent.

Some conversations, some arguments are meant to be lost.

Winning feels great at the moment but at what cost?

Putting someone else down so we feel up is the way of the EGO.

You have a quick line that you can get out and you will show that person who is more clever, but you are REACTING and creating a chain of events that is not intelligent.

When you become aware that it's better to tap into that higher level of intelligence and just be aware of your need to be so clever, you are able to pause all that winning.

Stop whining and whining, instead start being. Compassion is still passion. It takes much more to pause and experience than it does to go with every urge and get lost in the heat of the moment.

25

Often we forget how wonderful it just feels to allow the wind to blow in our face. We miss those gifts that are right in front of us, because we are so busy being clever to look important.

Looking important is not the most important thing.

Living your life by comparison is a recipe for lifelong failure and never really feeling fulfilled.

You cannot be successful comparing yourself to other people because there will always be someone that is more successful than you.

The reason why people are not satisfied with making money and they always want more is because they are being clever. People that are not satisfied are not being intelligent and becoming aware of the fact that they are enough. You are enough!

Often people tell me that they fear that if they are satisfied with what they have, that they will no longer have the drive to keep growing and they fear they will lose it all.

You do not lose it all by being at peace. You do not lose your hunger and drive by connecting with your inner energy.

You just get a different type of fuel that is not based on greed or need but based on purpose and meaning.

If you want to really find your purpose, if you want to find a fuel source that never runs out, you must stop being clever and start being more intelligent.

26

Stop thinking and overthinking and trying to win but instead being more aware.

Awareness is a place where things flow naturally.

If you are attracted to wealth, let it flow to you.

If you are attracted to love, let it flow to you.

When you try to take it, it runs away from you.

Let it flow and as it flows, take it. Let it come and as it comes pick it as it picked you first. Do not resist success.

Do not say that because YOU did not manifest it, because it was GIVEN to you that you do not WANT IT.

Sounds silly to see this in action. Some people have an EGO that does not let them receive gifts from other people. I see them fight about who will pay the bill. Who is the giver here and who is the receiver.

You probably heard that some people are more afraid of success than failure because it's easy to fail. You can control it, all you have to do is mess things up by overthinking, by being depressed, by being in your lower vibration state.

Success that comes from the inside is often not something that the EGO can wrap its thinking around. You cannot be clever, it's not even you. It just happens.

Networking is the manifestation of this type of acceptance. Givers go to meet other people and show them PRESENCE.

"How can I add value to your life?" No strings attached. This is powerful and its foundation is awareness.

Ask yourself how clever have you been trying to be?

Can you let go of looking so smart?

High Energy Observation: Write down where you want to be more clever in your life right now? Have you been comparing yourself with others? Notice the times you want to look smart or be better. Just notice and ask yourself whose agenda this is.

AWARENESS IS THE FOUNDATION OF PURPOSE

Finding purpose and meaning which is different from finding REASONS, takes a certain level of awareness.

When people go out on a mission to find their purpose, their energy source, as Viktor Frankel writes, "Man's Search for Meaning."

We are doing something active, we are searching or seeking.

Who is seeking? Why are you seeking? What are you hoping to find?

What do you really desire? Why do you want it?

You will not find happiness if you look for it? You will not get results if all you want is results.

Instead you need to go back to the source, the foundation of purpose.

Knowing your purpose is about being aware of your purpose. Not understanding your purpose so that you can feel good about yourself that you are ON PURPOSE.

The EGO creates purposes to be clever, to feel good, to look good, to please others and to feel important.

There is a deeper primary purpose that is what you need to tether onto so that you never lose your fuel and you do not get burned out.

Awareness is unlimited, you never get tired of being aware. It's just something that you layer onto like a filter.

It does not take more effort. It's effortless to be conscious.

We also effortlessly forget that we have that feature and we get lost in a secondary purpose. But without the foundation in the seat of consciousness, it's not really us being its source, it's our EGO doing.

You are the one who experiences all, and you need to remain aware as you live your life. This is your purpose, otherwise YOU do not exist.

You are not the one who argues, your mind argues.

You are the one who watches the argument unfold and decides to press pause, breathe, and experience the NOW. Seeing the bigger picture and realizing that we are all really connected, we are all really ONE being if we can all stay in the present moment.

Now ask yourself, how are you feeling right now?

High Energy Observation: Your purpose in life is to be aware. That's it. Being conscious takes no effort. If you need to make an effort, that's having an agenda. Notice where in your life you are struggling or doing something that takes so much effort and you are not liking it. Take a step back, breathe and remind yourself that this might be the EGO taking you on a ride.

HOW ARE YOU FEELING?

How do you know if you are being on purpose or if you are in your EGO? If you get lost, how do you know you are lost?

Well, our emotions are our GPS to know if we are being conscious, or if we are getting lost in EGO.

When you feel angry, resentful, bored, annoyed, frustrated, lonely or any emotion that is LOW VIBRATION, you must take a seat and explore those feelings without taking action.

You will realize that is not a place you want to linger, but hang out there and just see what caused these feelings.

Yes, you are right, it was your EGO blaming other people, blaming WHAT HAPPENED on those feelings.

You might be angry because someone wasted your time.

You might be resentful because someone keeps cutting you off.

You might be bored because you didn't even want to be here to begin with and it's not your fault.

You might be annoyed because everyone else is so annoying and you are so much smarter than everyone else.

You might be frustrated because you have to deal with the same things over and over and nothing is changing.

You might feel lonely because it's not fair that you are not loved and adored by someone who would make you their everything. Or you might come up with a million different reasons for these feelings.

All those reasons are thoughts about what happened and what might happen.

But they are not NOW.

Thinking those thoughts and focusing on them means you are not BEING present in the moment right now.

When you feel JOY, you are present. RIGHT NOW. You feel joy. When you feel PEACE, you are connected to the moment.

So how are you feeling? Really take a moment and explore and experience how you are feeling and see what comes up even if you do not label the feeling.

You might feel lost and not sure what you are feeling. That is a great place to be because if you are curious, you will see that you got lost because you lost awareness.

The EGO gets confused quickly and wants to have certainty. It uses it as a tactic to distract you and make you find a problem that you can complain about. It Makes you look for a desire that you can latch onto.

Seeking the truth through awareness will create more freedom. Reflect on your current state.

High Energy Observation: Feelings and emotions are part of us being humans but that's not what we are. Have you ever realized that emotions depict something that happened in the past(depressed) or will happen in the future(anxious)? If you are really in the present, your mind should be relaxed because you have nothing to worry about. So let us ask ourselves, Write down what you are feeling right now, in this moment, be descriptive and just observe what you feel without judgment.

DOING WILL NOT MAKE YOU FREE

We are so busy! What are we busy with? Who do you need to meet? What do you need to do?

More and more doing that we forget what really makes us free.

If only I had that house, that car, that friend, that skill, I would be free and fulfilled.

Then you get the house, you get the car, you get the friends, you get the skills and you ask yourself, "Is that all there is?"

Yea, you will not be fulfilled by doing. You will not be free by finding more things to do. There will always be more things to do.

The world will give you lots of chores if you seek them. You will be volunteered to do all types of things in your life.

Suddenly you realize that you no longer have time to do the things that really bring you joy and you are not compelled to do them because it will not be productive.

You know you feel guilty wasting time. You need to do more, so you can have more.
Having more will never make you free. The more you have, the more problems you have.

Instead of trying to do more, be more.

34

Who are you becoming?

Look at yourself and ask yourself if you can appreciate the light or do you see darkness.

Do you see how incredible you are, or are you rejecting what you experience?

If you HATE what you see, either transform it or just experience it which will allow it to automatically transform.

When we put light on the darkness, it transforms. There is no change, it's like the darkness was never there!

We no longer feel guilty for who we were, because who we were was a story that we made up with our mind.

You are who you are and you never changed. Be the light and keep shining. But Be!

High Energy Observation: Notice if you are more busy doing or being. You need the right balance but remember that most people only focus on doing because they are not aware that being is even a thing. This is a reminder that we are human beings, not human doings. Even if you're the busiest person on Earth, the question you can ask yourself is, how can I be more?

EGO THRIVES ON REACTION

Not every action is an action that is worth taking. Reaction is caused by another action.

Something happened as a RESULT of that.

You feel compelled to do something about it.

If someone yells at you, you might have the instinct to yell back, to fight back.

Your EGO will thank you for it because it is how you feel it. It can win the fight and get BIGGER.

Even if the EGO loses, it will convince and justify that what it did was the right thing to do and therefore become stronger and bigger.

When the EGO becomes bigger you lose more light, you lose more awareness and you become less conscious. You lose that connection with other people.

You start to feel alone and you become sad inside.

You make excuses that it's not your fault because THEY STARTED.

It's true, they did start, but your EGO reacted and you MUST take RESPONSIBILITY for your reactions.

Let's look at this wonderful word. "RESPONSIBILITY." Break it into two words.

Response ability.

It means the ability to respond. Not react.

You have a choice to behave in a more powerful way and remove what is JUST and FAIR but instead do what is intelligent.

Being clever you will want to win here. You will be COMPETITION and you will show them who is SMARTER and who is the IDIOT. If instead you are intelligent you will find a way where everyone wins. Not just you.

There is a possibility that EGO does not have to grow but it can be diminished and often it's through your own suffering.

Conscious suffering, which means reacting in a way that might seem like you are getting hurt and you are being vulnerable, will diminish your own EGO and sometimes also diminish and melt the EGO of the beings around you as a result.

I never understood why when you back down, other people back down too. Why don't they just keep going.? Why when a bug dies do you not keep smashing it.?

Because it's DEAD!

Because it has no power anymore, because it cannot annoy you anymore.

You lose your interest in the mosquito that is trying to bite you, so you let go and move on. Can you let go?

High Energy Observation: Where in your life are you being reactive or proactive? Being reactive is triggered by the ego while being proactive is about having intention and purpose. What part of your life do you need to be more proactive in?

PAIN WITH NO PURPOSE IS SUFFERING

What is pain? Is pain a feeling that you do not want to feel?

How is pain different from discomfort? What is emotional pain? Is pain a bad thing?

If you do not want pain, and you still have pain, and you can't get rid of the pain, you end up suffering.

Suffering is the state of not wanting what you are experiencing. You want what is happening not to happen and you are in a state of suffering.

You want what happened in the past not to happen.

You cannot change the past but you want to, so you are uneasy about it.

You are worried about the future and you suffer because you fear the future will not go according to how you want it to go.

If you do push ups, you feel pain after doing more than you're used to. That pain you might not call suffering because you are doing it with a purpose to become stronger.

When your pain has a clear purpose and it's not meaningless, you do not suffer from that pain. Instead it makes it bearable

The pain of childbirth would kill people if they did not have a strong purpose of creating life.

Think about the pains that you have in your life, the problems that you are experiencing right now that you DO NOT accept.

The ones that you feel are making you suffer.

To suffer is not to accept what is.

To suffer is not to enjoy the current moment.

Know that you have the ability to stop the suffering and redirect your energy to something more empowering.

Something that is more aligned with your internal purpose.

That pain you feel has a purpose.

To discover that purpose you first must accept the pain as part of your growth.

When you experience failure, you can call yourself a failure or you can take a step back and learn something from your failure that you can apply to the next time you get back up and try again with new enthusiasm.

The pain of losing is hard to swallow but it does not have to equal suffering if you can remain aware of the bigger picture. Everything is temporary in this world and the only thing that exists is this moment right now.

When you detach yourself from what you experience and realize that if what you experience is NOT YOU, then you must be the observer which is something that is connected to the unlimited power of the universe.

What happens in that moment is you have AWE. Allow yourself to feel it right now by taking a deep breath.

High Energy Observation: Do you have pain? Physical and emotional pain is inevitable but suffering is not. Find purpose in the pain you feel with the areas that have a clear external purpose. If you cannot find purpose in the pain, remember that you can always accept pain and notice it. The more you notice it, the less power it has over you. Pain is usually an action signal wanting to be noticed. Write down the pain in your life that you do not understand and that you still need to accept.

CHAPTER TWO: AWE

YOU ARE A MIRACLE

The fact that you are alive right now during the best time humanity has ever experienced and the fact that you are reading these words is a total miracle.

The fact that you can observe your thoughts and feelings, and that you can experience other beings that are indescribable is a miracle.

Acknowledge that all the experiences that you have right now have been given to you as a gift.

If you cannot see the gift, you are not looking.

Do not try to understand with your mind, instead experience with your being.

Be in awe of how miraculous you are because you are connected to the entire universe yet your body takes up very little space in the big scheme of things.

The awareness is what connects you with everything else that exists.

It's humbling to realize that all this time, you were a miracle that you may have missed because you were looking with your EGO and not with your being.

When you see your being as a miracle, you have a new sense of respect, honor and humility.

It allows you to see other people around you as a miracle too and you become much more tolerant to the things that usually trigger you.

After all you are just a speck of dust in the universe

High Energy Observation: You are a miracle. Write down how you might be taking that for granted? When was the last time you were grateful because you get to experience life while others do not?

JUST A SPECK OF DUST

Do you have any idea how big our galaxy is?

It is so big, it's almost incomprehensible.

Billions of stars exist and then we are here, a little human on planet earth, worried about some random thing that happened to us.

If you realize that you are a tiny speck of dust, you stop worrying so much.

Did you know that you have over a billion cells in your brain that correspond to the stars in the galaxy?

Your brain is connected to the whole universe.

You might be just a speck of dust but one that has awareness.

As far as we know, rocks, flowers and animals cannot comprehend the universe like we can.

We have special powers that only human beings have and yet we are just a speck of dust.

Planet earth is mostly water, your body is mostly water and your brain is mostly water.

High Energy Observation: Look at the problems in your life in the context of the whole world and then in the context of the whole universe. What comes up for you? Can you see your problems as insignificant compared to the universe?

WHAT DRAWS YOU IN?

Think about the things in your life that draw you in.

Pain will often attract us because we feel it the most.

It's like a loud bang, we automatically turn to the loudest noise.

As they say, the squeaky wheel gets the grease.

What is calling your attention, what is grabbing your awareness?

There is a deeper reason to become aware and observe what is drawing you in.

Be in awe of what has power over your attention automatically.

Why do you look when that passes?

Why did you think that particular thought?

Why is this person on your mind right now?

What problems are you focused on and why are you drawn to those problems?

Sometimes it's about just being with what draws us in that allows us to release that thing that is holding us hostage.

A child will cry for your attention and when you give them your full undivided attention they will often let go and not need it.

You might have a deep desire but once you get what you wanted, you no longer want it.

Realize that whatever is drawing you in has power and you can use that power or you can let the power of what is drawing you in to rule you with its own agenda.

How do you use that power?

Be with it and see where it goes, what it does, see what you experience and be a passenger.

You don't have to do anything with what you observe, just be with it.

You will see why you are drawn to it and you will see what needs to be done as a result but it will be automatic with no resistance.

True power comes when you go along with the forces that are natural, do not try to sail against the wind or swim upstream unless you enjoy the struggle.

If you are frustrated, see what happens when you let it flow and it starts to take you instead of becoming you, you are riding the wave.

You have the power to choose how everything that happens in your life will affect you.

High Energy Observation: Notice what is not working right now in your life and notice what is working and see if you can let go of controlling what is a struggle and instead focus on what is calling your attention. When you notice a pain, it often melts away when you breathe into it. Write down one thing that is not working and identify where the struggle is.

THE POWER INSIDE YOU

We all have unlimited power inside us but we cover up the power that we have because we want to feel important.

We want to avoid rejection and failure.

We want to feel accepted by getting outside validation.

Outside validation is very limited and it comes and goes.

Inside power is unlimited and you are in full control of it.

You must feel the power by being still. Everything is vibrating with intensity.

The more still you can get, the more alive you will feel.

At first you will be very uneasy because you are not used to feeling this power and you might be scared of it. Your EGO will not want to feel it, your mind will not allow you to just be.

Lots of excuses and reasons will come up. Allow them to just flow and do not resist them. Be with the reasons and excuses and find the power underneath them.

When you realize and become aware that you are the source of power deep inside you, it's an epiphany that comes suddenly and you are in total awe.

You have been looking for this power source all your life.

You have been seeking this power source in other people and from time to time you have gotten a glance at someone else showing their power.

The power inside you is attractive, it's confident, it's steady and it's always available to you.

But you must know it's there and allow it to be.

What stops this power is our fear and the EGO thrives in fear.

High Energy Observation: Notice what is taking your power away on the outside and start tuning into the power you have inside. Just notice your ability to influence the voice in your head and the feelings in your body. The ripple effect creates a reaction in the world. Notice the reactions on the outside that are caused by the shifts on the inside.

YOUR FEAR IS REALLY YOUR EGO

Ever wonder what FEAR really is? Why do we have it? Some people say that fear stands for False Evidence Appearing Real.

Fear is us thinking something is true but it is not really being true, yet it appears to be real.

What are you trying to protect really with your fear?

Fear is often trying to protect the EGO, that sense of self as other people see it.

The shell or facade that we have created on the outside.

A mother will want what's best for her children because she loves them but sometimes the child might rebel and the mother might be afraid that the child will be a failure and she will blame herself for his lack of discipline or lack of progress in life.

She will become depressed or angry because she wants her child to be successful. Yet she doesn't realize that her son is an independent person who is responsible for themselves as much as she is responsible for them.

They have to learn, grow, walk, fall and they are on their own journey.

Getting depressed because your child does not fit into what you call success is part of the EGO and it's the fear that you will not look good as a mother.

You might argue that it's not true, you just want your child to be HEALTHY and PRODUCTIVE, but if you desired that from love, you would not get depressed when it didn't happen.

Your desire comes from FEAR so you get angry when it doesn't happen.

Let go of the fear, let go of the attachment, let go of the EGO. Let it be.

That doesn't mean that you do not do your part.

That means that you remove the emotional charge from the RESULT.

You keep doing your job with love and enjoyment but if you do not get results, that doesn't hurt you emotionally.

We all know that results come from ACTION.

Fear stops action. Fear stops life. Doubt is the killer of progress. Fear creates doubt.

All the proof that fear brings is fake but it feels real.

That is why it's called an illusion, because it really looks like the REAL THING.

Your EGO exists only in the construct of illusion.

You have an illusion that you own something.

You fear it will be taken away from you.

Are you really a CEO? Are you really a Homeowner?

If you were a homeowner why when you die, you no longer own the home?

Do you own the land or can the government just take it if it needs it?

Everything is temporary, especially your feelings.

So why stress out about the desires of the EGO?

Why live in fear when you are aware that all this is nonsense.

The reason why we do it is because we forget and lose that awareness.

We get lost in our EGO, in our ROLES and we think that it's our primary purpose to control everything that happens with our environment.

Maybe your purpose is to experience what happens and not fear it.

What if you just allowed life to be the dancer and instead you were the dance?

What if you allowed life to be the water and you just flowed where it flows.

Going with the flow can be very enjoyable if you do not try to resist the flow. Fear makes you squirm, the EGO wants to control because it's scared of LOSING ITSELF.

You are not your EGO. You are not your ROLE.

You are the observer of your role.

Do a damn good job at your role but don't let it consume you.

When you feel powerless in your role, you need to find a way to reclaim your power.

Reclaiming your power is not about taking more action to change what happens, it's about realizing that what happens is a reaction.

Life is much better when you are not fighting with your ghosts.

Look around and ask yourself, where are you struggling?

What relationships are not working?

What aspects of your life are not the way they are supposed to be?

What does fear have to do with you not being where you think you should be?

People often think they need to be much further along than where they are right now.

They are afraid that they are not enough right now.

The truth is, you are where you need to be. Anything else is a lie because all there is, is where you are NOW.

Tomorrow you might be somewhere else, but often we don't take action to create that opportunity because we fear we might not get there.

Be with the internal energy, let the fear pass.

High Energy Observation: What fears do you have right now that you are holding on to that are really a part of your ROLE or EGO that are causing you frustration? Just write them down and notice them. See how they are stemming from fear and ask yourself how you can have a perspective shift with those fears. When you observe each role and write down the fears associated to that role, it becomes clear what the EGOs agenda is

CHAPTER THREE: AGREEMENTS

WHAT AGREEMENTS DO YOU HAVE IN YOUR LIFE?

We all have agreements we made, some we are aware of and some which we are not aware of.

These agreements often rule our life because they tell us how to use our attention.

When someone calls your name, do you give them your attention?

Does this happen consciously or automatically?

When did you agree that your name is Joe? Sally? David? Sarah?

Who decided to call you what you are called?

When you do not explore the agreements in our life we are bound by them and we do not even know what they are. We lack awareness about the agreements that were made for us that we blindly accept.

The agreement to take things personally when someone else offends us.

The agreement to make assumptions in our life that make us feel justified and right.

The agreement to not give our 100% when we feel like it's not worth the risk of failing so why try.

Some of us have these agreements and we will not create new empowering agreements unless we first accept that we are a slave to old agreements that no longer work for us.

A renegotiated agreement is not a broken agreement.

What agreements do you need to renegotiate with yourself and with the people around you? When we break agreements we are out of integrity, we feel out of place, we feel out of power.

Agreements are what allow us to be aligned.

Often we confuse a commitment with an agreement.

A commitment is about us, an agreement is what we are both committed to.

Agreements also must have consequences or exit clauses.

This way if you do not keep your agreement there is a price to pay.

We all agree that if we live in New York we cannot drive while under the influence and put peoples lives at risk. If we do it, and we get caught, we agree to pay a fine or go to jail.

By living in New York and getting a driver's license we are bound by those agreements.

There are natural agreements like gravity.

Those agreements are more like laws.

Everyone is bound to the same agreement.

Fire is hot, Water flows and gravity keeps us planted.

You may not agree to those natural agreements but because they are laws, you are bound to them even if you do not agree to them.

You must become aware and accept certain natural agreements about yourself.

One agreement is that you will give pain your attention.

When you feel pain, you will notice it.

The more the pain, the more the attention you give it.

Even if it's a simple pebble in your shoe. Try to walk a mile and forget that the pebble is in your shoe.

All you will think about is the rock in your shoe.

If you know this, you can work with this.

If you know your agreements, if you know the laws and the rules you play by, you can leverage these agreements and create the state of being that you want to create for yourself.

Having agreements that align with your purpose is powerful because you can use your agreements to fulfill your purpose.

You want to feel complete, fulfilled, at peace, in flow.

Money can't buy those feelings.

In the book "The four agreements" the author speaks about the agreements that you want to proactively create to have a life that has less drama in it.

The EGO creates drama and if we are aware of these 4 agreements we will avoid getting lost in the desires of the EGO and live a more empowered life.

Be Impeccable with your word. Do not make assumptions. Never take things personally. Always give your best.

People that subscribe to these agreements have more peace and don't get lost in their EGO as often as people who are not aware that these agreements exist.

What agreements will you be creating in your life?

How will your agreements impact your level of awareness, and help you fulfill your purpose?

Now that you know your agreements, it's time to set boundaries.

High Energy Observation: Explore the agreements you have in your life that you are aware of. Write down the agreements you have in your life that you just take for granted and do not think about often. Write down the agreements you need to create with other people. Write down the agreements you need to make with yourself.

THE BOUNDARIES YOU MUST HAVE IN YOUR LIFE

The EGO does not like control or limits on itself.

The EGO likes to control what happens but it doesn't not like it when other EGOs control what happens with it.

Do you like when people tell you what to do?

Do you like to be bossed around by someone who you do not respect, by someone who is on a lower level than you? Do you like to be triggered? How does it feel to be manipulated?

Being that you cannot change other people, instead creating boundaries is a powerful way to allow people to know where you stand.

Countries have physical boundaries around them. Some even put up walls.

To enter someone's land means to agree to their rules.

The question is have you established rules and communicated them or are you assuming everyone knows what your rules are?

Ground rules allow us to operate at a higher level.

When you create boundaries with yourself, you are setting a standard with what is acceptable.

Know and understand what your limits are for yourself and for your relationships.

Think about the physical, emotional and mental limits as well as spiritual boundaries that are acceptable.

Tuning into your feelings is the key to understanding where we are letting go of our boundaries.

Healthy boundaries are a sign of self respect so give yourself permission to create healthy boundaries and communicate them.

Feelings that cause stress, resentment or any other disempowering feelings are often caused by a lack of honoring boundaries.

When it comes to boundaries with yourself, think about the areas of your life that you want to improve, finances, productivity, organization, mental and emotional state.

One of the boundaries that I created is that I turn my phone off before I go to sleep so I don't use it while I sleep or first thing in the morning.

Instead I am proactive in the morning and focus on more empowering behaviors.

Ask yourself what boundaries do you need to create and whom do you need to create them with. Honor your boundaries, show respect and you will feel more aligned with your purpose.

High Energy Observation: What boundaries are people crossing in your life right now? Where do you need to create a few boundaries and communicate those boundaries with other people and with yourself? Write them down and think about what boundary changes need to be created in your life.

RESPECT AND HONOR, WHAT IT MEANS

There are times where people do things that make you feel like they don't deserve respect.

I even had a person tell me "I am not a respectable human being."

What do you do with that?

For me I choose to be with it.

Honor it and observe that statement.

The difference between respect and honor is that respect is about holding someone or something to a high regard.

When you have respect for someone you treat them differently than if you do not respect them.

Honor is about recognition of the importance of value in something or someone.

You can honor someone whom you have a hard time respecting.

When you separate the two, you are able to show more compassion for people and things in your life that cause you pain.

For example, you might not be able to honestly respect your parents if they are abusive to you.

We all know stories of people who have parents that are dysfunctional.

Some parents mentally, verbally but others physically too.

You can honor them for being your parents but that doesn't mean you need to interact with them if the interactions are unhealthy.

You can create boundaries and have agreements with yourself and with them that you uphold with honor and dignity.

When you tune into your awareness and you stop letting your EGO view the people in your life with judgment, you have the capacity to honor people.

Honor will often lead to a certain level of respect. When you respect and honor someone, you are admiring something about them.

If you have someone in your life that you cannot respect, ask yourself what about them are you labeling.

You might have someone who you feel wronged you and you blame them for what they did.

 As long as you do not forgive and you hold on to that resentment, you are in your EGO and you will not be able to honor them.

It feels empowering to honor someone for just being a human being.

Honor your parents for bringing you into this world. Honor your partner for running your business with you.

Honor your spouse for coparenting with you.

Find ways to honor and appreciate and you will have a new level of self respect.

Forgiveness is the key to being aware enough to honor and respect.

High Energy Observation: Who In your life do you have a hard time respecting? Think about how you can honor people that you do not agree with or that you do not respect. Write down your own definition of honor and respect. Do you honor and respect yourself?

FORGIVENESS IS A HIGH PERFORMANCE TOOL

Is it fair to forgive someone who wronged you?

Especially if they did not properly apologize?

Forgiveness is powerful because once you understand how it works you can use it to perform on a higher level.

When you forgive someone for doing something you are not condoning what they did.

You are not saying, "It's ok, that you did this or that, or that you said this or that."

Forgiveness is not about them.

Forgiveness is letting go of the need and ability to punish the person that wronged you.

When you forgive you do not wish what happened did not happen.

You stop wishing things were different and you let go of that bitter resentment.

Resentment is like the poison that you take, hoping that the other person dies.

When you are full of resentment, you are the one suffering.

69

When we are in our EGO we cannot see the resentment but we can feel it in our bodies.

We become tense, we get triggered, we are uneasy.

Resentment is stored in our physical bodies and it weighs us down.

We store it because what happened is too painful to experience so we put it away for later.

The urge to get revenge means that you still have resentment and the need to punish yourself or someone else for what they did to you.

Realize that no one did anything to you, people do things and we make it mean they did it to us.

You cannot change what happened.

You can only change the story you tell yourself about what it means.

Do not try to change the past, because the past is a story your EGO holds onto to justify its agenda.

The more you are tuned into the present moment, the more you will be anchored in reality instead of floating around in your mind.

You cannot experience life when you are viewing everything through the lens of resentment.

Clear up the foggy glass by letting go of the need to change what happened.

Accept what happened as something you cannot change.

When you accept the present moment and you let go of resentment you are able to have more integrity with your words and actions.

High Energy Observation: Who do you need to forgive in your own life? What do you need to forgive yourself for? Write down a letter of forgiveness to those that you must forgive while at the same time remembering that you are not condoning what happened. See how it feels to no longer have resentment towards other people and yourself.

WHAT IS INTEGRITY?

When you have integrity, things work the way they are supposed to work.

When you are out of integrity things break down and stop working.

Do not confuse morality and integrity.

Morality is about the difference between good and evil, right and wrong.

Integrity is not about right and wrong, it's about will something work or not work.

When the spokes on a bicycle wheel are bent or missing, the wheel is no longer round.

A round wheel is not BAD, it's just out of integrity.

A wobbly wheel will not really work very well. Your bike will fall and you will not get very far.

That doesn't make it right or wrong. We are not judging a wheel that is out of integrity, we are just noticing that it's the reason it doesn't work.

If you want the wheel to work, just adjust the spokes or add the missing spokes and BOOM, your wheel now has integrity and it works.

There is nothing wrong with you if you lack integrity with your word, it just means that your word loses power.

When you do not keep your word, you cannot create with your word.

Words create agreements, words create boundaries, words create the reality we experience. When those words lose integrity we lose the power they have.

Keeping your word means doing what you say you will do.

Being who you say you will be.

Realize that if you do not have results you want right now in your life, you are just out of integrity with the laws and agreements that are stopping you from getting what you want. It takes a certain level of awareness to see the lack of integrity we have instead of blaming others.

Once you realize that, you know exactly what needs to get done.

The EGO is a dysfunctional part of us that lacks integrity. It lies, cheats and robs us of our sense of self and tells us we are not beautiful, judges us and blames us and makes us feel guilty.

When it's done making us feel less than we are, it finds others to judge, blame, shame, call names, etc.

Be honest with yourself and ask yourself where in life are you missing integrity and what can you do to get back to integrity so you live a life that has more power and freedom.

High Energy Observation: Write down the difference between integrity and morality for yourself and see where in your life you are missing integrity and thereby not getting the intended results you are looking for. Think about what needs to happen to repair broken integrity in your life with your relationships and with yourself.

DO YOU REALLY HAVE TO GET WHAT YOU DESIRE?

There are two ways to experience unhappiness.

The first way is to want something and not get what you want.

The second way to experience unhappiness is to want something and get what you want.

Yes, desire is not the answer to happiness.

Someone once told a Guru "I want happiness, how do I get it?" He replied, "Remove the I and the want and you will have happiness."

When you have EGO, and you have desire, it looks for problems.

Every problem you have right now is one that you created with your EGO and your desire.

Do you consider having a mortgage a problem? Well, didn't you desire to buy a house like the Jones next door? What about that car payment?

Every problem you have from your relationships to your finances to your own personal wellbeing, is a problem that you can solve but that will just lead you to the next problem.

Desire exists, and when you can experience desire without acting on it right away you get a deeper understanding of the agenda that your EGO has.

If you are looking for physical pleasure. Are you in control of it?

Does it make you feel good after you binge on the box of cookies? Enjoy one cookie, not the whole box.

Yes, you are allowed to have pleasure but don't confuse desire with obsession.

When you are obsessed with a desire it does not let you think, you compulsively are being taken over by your EGO and you are being dysfunctional.

Only when you reflect on your actions later do you ask yourself, what was I thinking?

Maybe you want to enjoy a drink to loosen up but you do not have to finish the bottle of wine.

Having integrity, agreements, boundaries, understanding your EGO and being aware of what is really going on in your life will allow you to accept your current situation.

When you accept your situations and you have AWE for how incredibly amazing you really are, you can optimize your agreements and live a life that is on purpose.

High Energy Observation: Write down your desires and ask yourself which ones you are obsessed with and sometimes regret spending too much time chasing those or the ones that are in conflict with your values, goals and vision for who you want to be. Ask yourself how your desires that have negative consequences in your life are connected to your Ego.

CHAPTER FOUR: SKILLS

DO YOU KNOW HOW TO FOCUS?

One of the most overlooked skills that humans have is the skill of Focus.

Some people get confused and think it's a talent.

You might say that Focus is not one of your strong suits.

When you make focus a priority you can learn how to become better at focusing.

When you focus, you get rewarded with traction.

A simple rock can be turned into a gem with focused polishing.

A diamond can only be cut with a laser made of focused light.

The times that I achieved the most in my life, are the times that I focused.

The EGO will not let you focus because it is afraid of putting all its eggs in one basket.

Focus means saying that you know what is most important, you are confident and have no doubt that where you are right now is where you need to be.

79

You let go of everything else that might take away from your focus.

The more you focus, the more you see the benefits of focusing.

The better you will get at focus as a skill.

When you focus, you see things more clearly.

You start to hear things you never heard before.

Maybe something has been said to you dozens of times but you never focus on the message.

Because you were out of focus.

Doubt leads us down a blurry road and when we keep seeing everything as blurry, we start to think that this is the new normal.

We no longer know who we are, we are out of touch and out of focus.

Learning to focus takes courage.

Fear will not let you focus, it will get your mind thinking of all the WHAT IFs that are possible.

Focus means allowing your mind to be like water.

A focused mind can be disturbed but will come back to its original state once the disturbance passes.

Like throwing a pebble into water, you will see ripples but depending on the size of the pebble that is now many ripples you will see and eventually it subsides.

Learning that focus is a skill and applying yourself to master focus will help you get more done in life.

High Energy Observation: Reflect on your ability to stay focused and think about where in your life you need to be more focused. Start a concentration practice to become better at focus and concentration. The more you focus, the more focused you will become. Write down your relationship to focus and how you can improve it.

WHAT RESOURCES DO YOU HAVE?

You do not need more resources, you only need to become aware of all the resources available to you right now and leverage them.

First take an inventory of your resources.

Think about the skills you have, the people in your life, the environment that you have the honor to be in.

Once you take stock of your resources you can ask yourself how well are you already leveraging those resources?

An investor once told me that he would never invest in a business that wants to use the money to operate the company.

I asked why, he said because they are not using their resources properly.

Investments are here to grow the company not to operate it.

That's a loan.

That got me thinking about the debt we get ourselves into because we mismanage our resources.

We lean on other people for things we have inside ourselves.

You have the capacity to love yourself yet you give up your self respect, time and energy to get other people to maybe show you some love.

Your ego starves for things you already have.

You might have enough money, but your EGO wants more because your friend has more than you, so you think you will feel complete if you have more.

More will not make you feel complete, understanding how to leverage what you have to get you where you need to go is much more important.

You have incredible skills, talents, abilities, experiences, connections and ideas that are unique and powerful.

How are you using them right now to support you on your vision?

Instead of thinking that you need to LEARN more to BE more, realize that you are enough.

If you are compelled to learn a new skill, by all means learn it but do not let it STOP you from living your best life thinking that if you get in DEBT you will be saved.

I know far too many people that go to college to make their parents happy and end up in major debt and they do not have the skills they need to earn a good livelihood.

Do you know someone who is not leveraging the resources they have because of fear?

Do you know someone who has people in their life, offering them opportunity but they do not want to take up those people on the opportunity because of their own EGO?

Think about this.

High Energy Observation: Where in your life are you looking for more resources but are not finding them? Write down what resources you already have that you can start leveraging better. It could be people, skills, money, access. Be creative and write down your resources.

THE SKILLS THAT EGO CREATED

Your EGO has been a gift all these years. Even if you did not know it was there and it DROVE you, do not feel bad.

It has done some amazing things for you in your life.

For some people, their lack of awareness has compelled them to grow wealth, for others their lack of awareness has created powerful persuasion skills.

I know someone who always wanted to be famous, he learned how to be a professional actor, a professional musician, a dancer, etc.

When he discovered that his desire to be famous was his EGO and it was not allowing him to be famous, he felt bad that he was so driven by his EGO all these years and worried about everything that his EGO stopped him from enjoying.

When he became connected to his essence he stopped worrying about that immediately.

He realized that his EGO created powerful skills that without the EGO would have never been created.

Skills that he LOVES and that bring him enjoyment.

If you have skills that your EGO created, honor those skills and use them but do not let them take away your awareness.

Do not get lost and think that YOU ARE your skills.

Remember that skills are a gift that you can use to create in this world.

Do not confuse the tools with the carpenter.

To a hammer, everything looks like a nail.

You are not a hammer, you are the one who decides where to focus the hammer and how to use it.

You might have skills that you want to learn, languages that you might want to master.

Keep mastering new skills and honor the ones that were created subconsciously under the influence of the EGO.

Make sure that you are learning skills for the right reasons moving forward.

Do not let your need to be IMPORTANT or your FEAR of not being enough to be the driving force behind your new skill creation but instead allow your source of inspiration to come from love and enjoyment.

When you allow your skills to flow from LOVE you will see how much more seamless skill creation becomes and you will take your skills to a whole new level with more passion and more enthusiasm.

Can you appreciate the skills that you created with your EGO?

High Energy Observation: Make a list of your SKILLS and see how your EGO created them. Observe them and see the ones you are celebrating and the ones you need to celebrate more and use for your higher purpose.

WHAT ARE YOU DRAWN TOWARDS?

When you look at a fire, you see the fire is always pulling upwards, seeking oxygen and striving to return to its source.

The fire thirsts for something more than just burning on a wick, it is drawn towards something greater.

You are a fire. You are being drawn towards your source.

You are connected to something that pulls you in.

Are you aware of the things that are drawing you in?

What are you compelled to do?

Do you love music and are compelled and drawn to it?

Do you love to write and are drawn to communicate with the written word?

Are you drawn to science or business or spirituality?

What draws you in is connected to you and what brings you joy will keep you energized.

There will be times where you will be afraid of following the path you are being called to follow.

You will run away from it and it will keep calling you back.

The more you resist this path the more it pulls you in closer and you might feel guilty or ashamed or frightened to follow this path.

A path of leadership, a path of passion, a path of exploration that your EGO will not want you to take because you want to stay inside your comfort zone or because you are being influenced by outside sources that have their own agendas.

To know what you are drawn towards you must get quiet.

Remove all the outside distractions and noise and listen.

No need to take action other than becoming aware of what is drawing you in and experience it.

When you experience the signs you are going to get more clarity and with more clarity you will have more motivation to take action.

Action takes courage because you still have FEAR that will stop you.

Courage means taking action in spite of fear.

If you did not have fear, you would not need courage.

There is a reason you are being drawn to it, explore the purpose and discover your destiny.

High Energy Observation: Write down what you keep being drawn towards and how it aligns with your external purpose and your mission in life. Notice how it comes up for you.

YOUR WEAKNESS IS REALLY A STRENGTH

Your EGO is always telling you where to focus.

Often it's on your weaknesses.

How much time are you spending thinking about the things that you are just not good at?

Most people I know would rather fix the parts of them that are not good instead of focusing on the strengths and doubling down.

I want to make you aware that your weaknesses are ONLY there because of a complimenting strength that you developed.

We are born with balance and because of our EGO we get out of balance.

We are compelled to become very powerful at one thing which creates what someone else views as a weakness somewhere else.

Those that are great at starting things are often not that great at finishing or consistency.

Those that are great at finishing or consistency are often stuck when they don't have a starter in their life.

I know a few people that are amazing at operating businesses but they are missing a visionary so they lack opportunities that allow them to grow.

They feel bad about their "weakness" and they wish they were more out of the box thinkers.

On the flip-side there are many visionaries that are very out of the box thinkers but they are not great at operating a business or making an idea a reality so they keep coming up with new ideas and none ever really take off.

They feel bad about their "weakness" and they wish they had more consistency.

Personally, I am one of those visionaries, for the longest time I spun my wheels trying to be better at managing projects.

Time management books, procrastination, dealing with my lack of integrity and focusing on my weaknesses.

I did not really feel alive till I let go of the idea that I have a weakness and instead focused on my strengths.

For me the solution was finding people in my life that complimented my strengths with their strengths and that allowed me to stay in my lane.

My EGO still bugs me about my weaknesses but I remind the EGO that I have those weaknesses as a result of my strengths and that is the only way I can be who I am, so put it to rest and enjoy your strengths.

Get complete with who you are and stay aware of what you are capable of.

High Energy Observation: Have you recently made a list of your weaknesses? Take a moment to look at all your weaknesses and see how they are the opposite of a strength that you have. You might be terrible at details but you might be great at the big picture. You might not be great at the big picture but it's because you understand how to deal with the details well. Think about your weaknesses and stop feeling guilty, instead celebrate them and create systems to support you where you need support.

LEARN TO BREATHE AGAIN

Are you breathing right now?

Breathing always happens all day and night.

As long as we are alive we are breathing.

Yet most people including myself had no idea how to breathe.

In from your nose, out from your mouth is much more effective at centering you than in from your mouth and out from your mouth.

The most important thing that all our cells need is oxygen and when we breathe like most people breathe, we get stressed out via the lack of oxygen in our blood.

Taking just three deep breaths can change your mood, your state of being and allow you to get more present.

Focus on your breath for 30 seconds and see what happens, you might feel a tingling sensation in your head.

You might feel a muscle that you have been storing lots of tension in starting to loosen up.

There is nothing you need to have or to do for you to become one with your breath, just let go and notice your breath.

The noticing of the breath automatically makes us breathe more naturally. Learning to breathe better is about learning to let go of the need to control but instead observing.

When you have a longer deeper breath you get more from each inhale and you are able to perform at a higher level.

Become aware of your breathing and allow the breath to center your being.

High Energy Observation: Take a moment and notice your natural breath. Is it from your nose or mouth when you do not think about it? Take a deep breath in from your nose and see where you feel it. Observe your breath and see what it feels like in all the parts of your body.

COMMUNICATION IS ABOUT LISTENING FIRST

Are you really listening or are you listening for a way to prove your agenda?

When we communicate with other people we by default communicate through the lens of what's in it for me.

How can I make sense out of all this to help me achieve my goals?

Do you listen to be heard or do you listen to really understand and experience what is being communicated?

Your ego does not allow us to hear what is being said outside of the context of how it applies to you.

Ever been told, don't make it about YOU, this is about me.

Or don't make it about ME this is about you.

Ever get lost in your own thoughts while someone else is talking to you or you are reading a book or watching a video and you forget you are there.

Your ears are still hearing what is going on but your mind has left the building.

Learning to stay present in the conversation, staying in the communication and focusing on listening is a key skill that when practiced can give us new levels of awareness and connection.

How well are you equipped to listen?

What conversations do you strategically check out of?

Communication is important with other people but it's also important with yourself.

Learning how to understand what you are feeling, learning to observe your thoughts is really important.

Communication is a skill that can be learned, you can learn how to write more effectively, how to speak more effectively and ultimately it will help you have clearer thoughts and with clarity comes motivation.

High Energy Observation: Observe how you listen to when other people are talking. Do you have an urge to respond before they finish speaking because you think you know what they are going to say? Stop yourself and keep listening. Write some notes down with what you observed that you would have missed if you did not listen actively.

CHAPTER FIVE: SOLUTIONS

WHAT IS YOUR ENDGAME?

Begin with the end in mind they say but do you really care about the end?

You want success NOW! Not time for the end. No patience for waiting.

The reason you want to think of your endgame it's because to have a purpose we must first observe what we want to end up with.

Before we begin on a journey we must understand where we want to go so that we can leave prepared.

Measure twice and cut once because when you measure you can see things you didn't see before. When you wing it, you get random results but when you measure you know what you are aiming for.

Life punishes the vague and rewards the specific, so be specific with what you want to get out of life.

What does your ideal day look like?

Remember, I said Ideal day, not perfect day

High Energy Observation: Write down what your current day looks like and create a version of your ideal day. Compare what needs to change and optimize one thing from your current day to make it more ideal.

PROCESS VS PRODUCT GOALS

When you are defining your external purpose, it's important to realize that actions and results are two different things.

Most people like to measure results.

How much weight did I lose, or how much money did I make but results are not actionable.

You cannot do something to change results in the present moment.

While it's very important to measure results and see where you are, it's more important to make sure you are measuring activity.

Action and activity is the goal.

When you want to lose weight, you need to measure what you eat, how much you move, how much water you drink.

When you are growing a business you can measure sales but you also have to measure how many calls and conversations you had and how many emails you sent out to new potential customers, etc.

Measuring the right goals will help you stay on track for accomplishing your external purpose and getting more of the right things done.

99

When you know you are getting the right things done you are able to stay more present and do your tasks with more enjoyment and enthusiasm.

Your internal purpose is to stay aware and conscious while you do anything that you are doing.

Feel the connectedness and aliveness of the universe in what you are doing right now. Living both your internal purpose and external purpose together you will feel like you are grounded and become unstoppable.

Do not make the mistake to get so focused on the results that you start having fear that your goals are too big or that you might fail.

Focusing on product goals is the reason why so many people have goals but do not take action.

When you learn the difference between the two types of goals and the two types of purposes you will know exactly where to put your focus and have more progress while remaining aware.

High Energy Observation: Write down your process goals and your product goals and start measuring your process goals while detaching yourself from the results so you take consistent action.

SUCCESS IS PERSONAL STOP COMPARING

When you stay focused on your actions instead of your results you also stop comparing yourself to everyone else.

When we think about our goals and success, we often compare our own success to the success of other people.

That is a recipe for disaster because your purpose is very different from someone else's purpose.

If you define your external purpose based on someone else's purpose you will be lost because you are going down the wrong path.

Do not wish things were different, instead transform into the person who knows, who sees, who is and BE!

Your EGO wants you to chase other people's dreams and desires, these are not your dreams.

These are dreams that you hope will give you a sense of importance in the eyes of others.

You being rich and famous will not help you feel fulfilled and at peace if that is not your purpose.

The opinions of other people are none of your business and if you try to please all the fans, you will not be playing the game.

The players in the game are trained not to pay attention to the opinions of the fans yelling from the sidelines.

Some will like you, some will hate you but you are busy playing the game and their opinions will never affect your level of performance.

You need to stay centered and in the game of your own life.

Being aware that success is personal, you can define anything you want as success.

For me it was building a million dollar business and teaching others how to do the same.

I didn't see someone else do it and then want it, no one in my family ever did that.

None of my friends did that.

I just pursued what I knew that I wanted and what I felt was my destiny.

What does success look like for you?

If no one else mattered, not your parents, friends, society , etc.

If no one was looking and no one cared, what would you see yourself as doing and creating?

What brings you JOY?

What can you give 100% of your attention to and be fully in with?

That is what you will be attracted to and what will draw you into success.

High Energy Observation: Where in your life are you comparing your success to the success of other people in your life? Write down what brings you joy and how that is different from what you consider success.

YOUR WHY IS EXTERNAL

Your internal WHY is to be grounded in the NOW, just experience and be one with everything that is happening NOW.

When you hear about this WHY this purpose that people try to tap into for motivation because they say people care about your WHY not your WHAT or your HOW.

Your WHY is external, it's based on language.

Anything that you can define with words you can observe and it's not you.

People think that they are their WHY, you are not your WHY. You are the one who observes and chooses to focus on your WHY.

Learning where you feel success is important and there are actually 9 ways that people feel success.

Finding your way of feeling success is important because it will help you find enjoyment and freedom.

Realize that it's external and it's easy to get sucked into believing that this is who you are.

We all get so engrossed with doing that we forget to BE.

This is totally normal, this is why books like this help us remind ourselves to be more present and more in the NOW.

Pull yourself out of your external WHY and just observe everything around you.

Your EGO might not let you do that but accept that too.

Accept the way that you do not want to pull yourself out and that itself is healing.

When you resist, you persist, so no resisting, just noticing.

Creating a vision, goals, having a strong WHY that you resonate with is important but know that it's all external and it does not DEFINE who you are on the inside.

You will always remain pure consciousness.

High Energy Observation: Observe who you are and how it's different from what you want to accomplish. Notice that anything that you attach language to is different than experiencing but when you experience words do not define what you experience.

CREATE A VISION THAT CHANGES

Do you have a crystal clear vision in your life?

Do you know where you want to go, what you want to do?

Who do you want to become?

The reason why most people don't have a clear vision is because maybe you created a vision in the past and you were let down.

You figure, why create a vision that might have to one day change.

I will feel like a failure, better not having a vision to begin with and I won't fail.

The anticipation in our life is what brings us excitement, you want to feel excited about something that you look forward to.

You also do not want to feel the dread and the pain of expectation and not getting what you expected to get, what you feel you are entitled to.

Your EGO will scream, NOT FAIR! I earned this, this is mine! I was expecting this.

You end up taking it personally and it makes you anxious that someone or something is taking advantage of you.

Sometimes you even think you are being punished.

The only thing that is punishing you is your own mind, your own EGO is punishing you into thinking that you are being punished.

No one is punishing you, no one is even considering you right now, because YOU are the one who is aware of your thoughts and that YOU are busy focusing on the EGO instead of the big picture.

Creating a vision that can change is a powerful way of deciding to anticipate with all your heart yet know that if your vision doesn't come to fruition that you have the ability to create a NEW vision that aligns with your new circumstance.

I know a woman who had a vision to live in an apartment that the government paid for and live off welfare and never have to worry about money or food or shelter.

One day her son came to visit her and told her that he won the lottery and was a multi millionaire, he said he bought her a brand new home and stocked it for her.

She started getting nervous and angry because she felt like her vision was crumbling, she cried "Now I will lose all my benefits" Let go of what was and see NEW opportunity in what is.

Only by being tethered in the now can you create a vision in the future that does not have the past associated with it.

How do most people create a vision?

They look into the past and they take elements of the past and decide to build on that for the future. Because they feel like if they did it in the past they can do it in the future.

I'm telling you that your past does not equal your future. If you can imagine it you can create it.

So create a new vision that can change and you will create more for your life.

High Energy Observation: Think about your vision from 5 years ago or 10 years ago for what you wanted out of life and see how it's different now. Realize that your vision can change but you remain the same. Write down your new vision for what you want to create in the next 10 years and see how that makes you feel.

CHAPTER SIX: SCHEDULE

DO YOU WANT MORE TIME?

You think you know what time is but time does not really exist. 5 minutes from now does not exist right now. 10 minutes ago does not exist either. It's in our mind.

Time is the way we measure the past and the future.

When you are in the NOW, time disappears.

There is no time right now.

10 years ago is what you remember, 10 years from now is what you imagine.

All that does not exist right now.

If you believe it once happened, that is your belief, not what is happening.

Is it possible that the future might not happen?

Is it possible that you remember something that didn't happen? Yes, you know very well that our memories are imperfect but we act as if we are our memories.

Do not use time as an excuse, use time as a tool.

You can use the idea of time to measure and coordinate with other people.

You can use time to be part of society and to make sure you don't miss important moments.

Remember you cannot manage time, you can only manage your priorities, which means what you plan on doing at any given moment.

You have to decide how you will spend the present moment, the NOW.

If you try to stop the clock or turn back time, that's not something that will give you any satisfaction because you will be missing the now.

If you worry about a future that you do not want to happen, you are giving it more power.

The best place to spend your "Time" is in the now.

Not yesterday and not tomorrow.

Learn to master time to be able to master the present moment and get in the NOW.

Learn to prioritize and plan because if you fail to plan, you might as well plan to fail.

To be successful you must use strategy but to be fulfilled you must be in the now.

A mentor once told me that success without fulfillment is the ultimate failure.

To me that means, if you create a strategy and you accomplish your goals but you are not in the now, you missed the opportunity for true success.

Do you have your priorities clear in your mind?

Do you know how to use time instead of allowing time to use you?

High Energy Observation: If you think that you need more time then you need to rethink your priorities in life. We all have the same 24 hours in the day. Focus on the NOW because NOW is infinite. Write down what your relationship with time is and your relationship with the present moment.

WHAT DOES SOMEDAY MEAN?

I looked through the whole calendar looking for "someday".

I found Sunday, Monday, Tuesday but I couldn't find "someday".

Why are you telling me that someday, you will begin doing what you love?

Why are you committed to starting someday, when the time is right?

Turns out that "someday" doesn't exist.

Someday is an excuse.

Someday is a placeholder for not today. Not now. Possibly never.

When you put something in the someday category you are giving yourself permission not to do that thing today but you are also saying that you do not know when you will engage with it.

That leaves an open loop in your time, unless you redefine what someday means.

To me someday means, I will re-evaluate this in the future. Not now, not today, not tomorrow.

I like the sound of the idea, but I have other priorities now.

Someday means NO to doing this now, I do not want to forget about this idea because it might be useful for me to remember it.

I do have a "someday" bucket but I will not regret not doing anything I put in the someday bucket.

If you might regret it, instead of putting it in the "someday" bucket, set a date to this idea.

If you want to write a book, plan a date in the future when you will begin writing the book.

If that creates too much pressure, you can always change the date.

Remember a negotiated agreement is not a broken agreement.

Someday is a great tool if you don't use it like most people use it, an excuse not to do what you love today.

If you find yourself saying that SOMEDAY you will be happy, you are missing out on life today.
Do not put off happiness for someday.

Remember that "someday" does not exist.

If it's important either do it today or set a date in the calendar.

What gets scheduled, gets done.

High Energy Observation: What have you been pushing off? Write down a list of some day projects, ideas and tasks and pick the ones you want to actually accomplish and set a BY WHEN date.

WHY THE PAST HOLDS US BACK

The past gets stored in your mind, in your body and in everything you have around you.

When you see something in your physical space, you automatically associate that thing with the past. Look at your clothing, your bed, your body.

You have a history with everything you observe that you consider yours. Where did you buy it? Who gave it to you? What experience do you have with those items?

All this happens automatically. If you want to create an empowering vision for the future you must become aware of the fact that your memories are faulty.

Your memories are often made of your imagination that matches what you want to believe to be true or what you NEED to believe to be true to hold up your current belief system.

If your past is made up of imagination, why can't you imagine a FUTURE that never existed and where there is no evidence that you can create that future for yourself?

Why can't you create a future where anything is possible? It's because the PAST that is STUCK in our minds and hearts hold us back and make history repeat itself.

It's said that humans have over 40,000 thoughts every day. Most of those thoughts are the SAME thoughts over and over. Our past keeps holding us back because it locks us up.

Only when we let go of the past and we are no longer attached to WHY this happened, or RESENTMENT or REGRET. Can we imagine a new vision that is not attached to the past?

Can you realize that the past is not real? Can you forgive? Can you let go? Can you move on? Can you imagine a future that is unrelated to the past?

If you cannot do that, you will be stuck in the same recurring life that most humans get stuck into. This is called the comfort zone. The pain we know is better than the pain we do not know.

So we settle for a mediocre life where we are not too happy but not too sad. Living mildly depressed is not living at all. It's barely surviving.

Free yourself of the past with awareness and a new strategy! Learn from your past and move on. An indication that you have something to learn from the past is that you cannot let it go yet.

High Energy Observation: Where in your life is history repeating itself? Write down things that you are not able to let go of and observe them. What part of your past are you having a hard time letting go of?

USE TIME AS A TOOL TO MEASURE ONLY

Time can be used as a tool to measure or can be used as an excuse to get lost with.

When we view time as REALITY we can get lost in the past or the future but all that is made up in our mind because all that exists is NOW.

The past is a STORY about WHAT HAPPENED, the future is a STORY about what WILL HAPPEN. We cannot predict the future because we have poorly made up memories about the past that we cannot trust to be accurate.

Do not discard time because TIME has a purpose. Time is meant to be used as a tool to measure what you are doing now.

How long you need to do things for. Who you need to meet where and when. Time is indeed more important than money because you cannot buy time, you cannot stop time, you can measure it but you cannot change it.

Like any tool you can only put it to use and what you do with it is your responsibility.

So instead of living in time, leverage time to measure everything you do. Most people do not measure what they do, they WING it.

The saying is Measure twice and cut once. Are you a master of time or is not having ENOUGH time driving you nuts?

I laugh when I hear people say they need an extra hour in the day. Because if we look at their calendar, often it's a mess or it's none existent. Anyone who measures time and has organized priorities will see that there is plenty of time to do what you need to get done.

Learn to use time the correct way and you will be able to accomplish your external purpose with more power and more freedom so that you can actually be in the NOW!

High Energy Observation: Are you measuring your time? How are you leveraging time as a tool vs an excuse? Where are you not having integrity with your time and relationship to time. Write down ways you need to improve your relationship with time and observe what comes up.

SPACE IS NEEDED TO GROW

A lobster is a mushy creature that lives in a shell. When the lobster needs to grow, it doesn't just grow its shell, it needs to hide under a rock and remove its shell so it can create the space to develop a bigger shell.

When you feel that you are stressed or you are in pain, maybe it's time to get behind a rock and remove your shell so that you can create more space.

Pressure is a sign that something needs to change.

You cannot ignore the pressure for too long because it builds up and eventually something breaks down.

Where in your life do you need more space? Sometimes it's in your relationship, sometimes it's a career or business situation.

How can you create more space in yourself and stop cluttering your time up with everything that will distract you from your pain?

Inspect your life and see where you have EXITS that are a distraction from your growth. For me it was WORK, I would work for 16 hour days just not to think about my problems.

For others it's alcohol, video games, drugs, or social media. Creating space means having room to breathe. Making time to reflect upon your situation so that you can create a better strategy for yourself.

When you do not make time to think, the thinking doesn't happen. You end up just doing and doing and doing the same old same old.

Creating space is scary because all these emotions start to come up. Fear, loneliness, boredom, frustration, anxiety or even anger.

It's important not to run away from those feelings or suppress them with food or exits that distract you but instead to be with the feelings and let them pass through you.

Let the pressure that you feel cleanse you and this too shall pass. When you allow enough space for growth, you allow space for new opportunities.

High Energy Observation: Are you resisting any pressure in your life or are you creating space for the growth that pressure creates? Where in your life are you feeling pressure and as a result you need to create some space for growth? Observe the pressure and see what type of growth you need to relieve the pressure.

SAYING NO TO DISTRACTIONS

For others it's alcohol, video games, drugs, or social media. Creating space means having room to breathe.

Making time to reflect upon your situation so that you can create a better strategy for yourself. When you do not make time to think, the thinking doesn't happen. You end up just doing and doing and doing the same old same old.

Creating space is scary because all these emotions start to come up. Fear, loneliness, boredom, frustration, anxiety or even anger.

It's important not to run away from those feelings or suppress them with food or exits that distract you but instead to be with the feelings and let them pass through you.

Let the pressure that you feel cleanse you and this too shall pass. When you allow enough space for growth, you allow space for new opportunities.

Many organizations reached out to me at once and it was overwhelming. I didn't want to say no to anyone. My coach told me that if I'm having a hard time saying no it's because I am not clear on what I'm saying yes to in my life.

So I made a list of charities and causes that I was passionate about and I focused my energies on those. It made me feel good to say NO to volunteer opportunities that were not in line with my vision.

I simply told them what I was up to and that I was focused on that. People respected the fact that I knew what I wanted and I had a purpose.

Want more respect? Want to be appreciated? Learn to say no with grace and class. Do not just say NO! But instead explain what you are focused on right now and why that is important to you.

Sometimes people will help you with your mission by communicating your mission to the distraction. A community leader asked me to come to his event as a guest and I told him that I am focused on networking and I am reserving my night for paid speaking engagements.

Instead of saying NO, I told him my purpose and my priorities. He thanked me for letting him know and offered to hire me to speak at his event.

Had I just said NO to yet another distraction I would have missed out on this opportunity. Knowing HOW to say no is more important than saying NO outright because that leads to opportunities that you did not think of yourself.

Remember that a renegotiated agreement is NOT a broken agreement. Look at your calendar and ask yourself, what meetings can you renegotiate to create more time and more space for what is really important?

What have you been doing that you can stop doing? What commitments can you remove from your life because they do not bring you enjoyment and you just said yes to them because you were afraid to say no or you didn't have a classy way to say no to those requests.

You will get requests every day that are not inline with your purpose. It's important not to ignore those requests but instead honor them.

Be with them and ask yourself the appropriate questions that help you identify if they are the right requests for you.

Once you see clearly that they are not aligned with your purpose you can decline and make suggestions for solutions that are helpful.

Sometimes a solution or some advice is better for the requestor than you just saying yes and enabling them out of EGO or fear of rejection.

The distractions that you have in your life are taking up more space than you are willing to admit or that you can even see. Often it takes asking a coach or peer to help you see the distractions that you are BLIND TO.

You can ask "What distractions do you see in my life that I cannot see?" You might get answers that you might not like to hear but just be with them instead of rejecting them.

Listen and see how interesting it is to see your life from the point of view of others. Can you make a list of distractions that you will consider saying no to?

High Energy Observation: What distractions are you having a hard time saying no to? Write down the things in your life that keep taking your attention. What do you need to do and who do you need to be for you to stay focused and say no to distractions?

CHAPTER SEVEN: AUTOMATION

WHAT HABITS DO YOU HAVE?

Now you have your internal purpose clear and you have more awareness. You also have your external purpose clear.

Knowing that whatever you are doing now is exactly where you need to be, while at the same time you have a clear vision for where you are going next.

How do you put your awareness and your strategy into action? It's called accountability. When you break down the word accountability, you have the ability to account or to measure.

You can only manage what you can measure, so if you want to be effective you must start by measuring your habits. Take into account the habits of thought, the habits of speech and the habits that make you have emotions that either lead to action or to fear.

The habitual emotions that are based in fear get you stuck in the powerless undesirable EGO driven actions that you want to transform.

Take stock of your thoughts and the voice in your head. Transform those thoughts into empowering thoughts. If you think "I am ugly." What do you think will happen when you look in the mirror, will you see how beautiful you are?

What do you think you will do with the compliments that people give you? Will you take them with grace and honor? Will you go out and be your best self or will you be stuck in your room to avoid the judgment?

Instead create a new habit of thought from "I am ugly" to "I am exactly the way I am supposed to be" to "I am beautiful" The voice in your head might fight you on that statement. Call you a liar, but that's the EGO trying to protect its thought habits.

Thought habits are powerful because they drive you mindlessly and no one knows they are there so no one can tell you about them to make you aware.

Your action habits are clear. If you don't brush your teeth, people will tell you that your breath stinks. But if you think in a way that makes you feel depressed, no one can remind you that you need to transform your thought habits but yourself.

Do not be down on yourself for having habits that are disempowering because you did not choose them, it just happened.

Once you are aware of all your thought, speech and action habits you can transform them by reprogramming your habits by leveraging awareness, strategy and accountability.

High Energy Observation: Make a list of the habits in your life that are empowering and the habits that you have that are disempowering that you want to reprogram. Just observe those habits and how they came to be and honor them for getting you to where you are today. Ask yourself if you are willing to replace them with new empowering habits.

HOW DO YOU WANT TO REPROGRAM YOURSELF?

You cannot solve a problem with the same level of awareness, than the level awareness that created the problem in the first place.

You need to be able to view the habits you want to reprogram objectively. Take a step back from voice and ask yourself what do I hear? Take a step back from your emotions and ask yourself, what do I feel?

Look in the mirror and ask yourself what do you see? If the answer sounds like guilt, shame, anger, sadness you have something to reprogram so you can see joy, freedom, happiness, vitality and peace.

Pain is an action signal and the first step to leveraging the pain is awareness that something is not the way you want it to be. Instead of blaming the pain, realize the source of the pain is lack of awareness and automatic habits of thoughts that got us to this problem.

When we use pain as a gift of awareness we can start to ease out of the pain and make small changes and shifts in our actions that will assist us and remind us to stay on course.

Remember that nothing really gets established in an instant, you need to plant the seed, then nurture it for a period of days, weeks and months to watch it thrive automatically.

If you have a vision of transforming your body, you must optimize the way you feel and think about your body. Know that you can do this and you have the power to create new habits and start with one at a time.

When I wanted to make running a habit, I simply made putting out my running gear the night before the habit. I used a trigger to help me get my running clothes on and when my running clothing was on me, I felt good and I pushed myself to run.

I did it long enough that it happens on its own now. If you want to have a more positive outlook, simply start praising the things around you and look for the good in your life each day and eventually it will become a habit.

Reciting affirmations are useful because we are creating new habits of speech that change our thoughts even if we do not believe them right now.

Over time, when you repeat something over and over even if it's a LIE we end up believing it and it becomes the truth to us. "I am enough, I am beautiful and I am worthy of love." "I have the power to change the world and be of service to the people in my life." "Good things happen to me and I live a blessed life."

What affirmations can you create to recite in your life and make them habitual thoughts?

High Energy Observation: Take a moment and think about the parts of your life that you want to reprogram. Write down those areas and make a commitment to starting the process of reprogramming yourself. It is simple yet it's not easy to do. Imagine yourself being the person you want to be. It will take some time but understand that you have the power and control over your programing.

WHAT DO YOU NO LONGER NEED TO DO?

Do you find yourself complaining often? Most people are not aware that they complain so much.

Now that you have the power to create any result in your life that you seek with the power of habit, you no longer need to complain.There is nothing that you cannot accomplish in this world because you understand that you can control your mind and your feelings.

You can shift your view and the world will shift and react to you. Do not spend so much energy on the things you do not want, do not give your power away to your fear, instead be with what you want to attract.

When speaking to people who say they want to change, I often see them saying that they TRY to change but no matter how hard they try, change does not happen. Trying is not the key to lasting change, it's automation.

Effortless habits that you create by shifting the SOURCE of the problem. Most people are trying to fight the symptoms in their life but if the source is still there, you are fighting an uphill battle.

If it's cold in your house, you can turn up the heat, start a fire, wear layers and bundle up but it's still cold because you left the window wide open.

Sometimes people take medicine to stop the headaches and they drink coffee to wake up but really they are just dehydrated and remain dehydrated because they are not aware that they do not have a habit of drinking water.

You no longer need to worry about those headaches when you realize that you are simply not drinking enough water, deal with the source of your problem and with the right automation you will no longer need to think about getting to your goal and you can be in the moment.

Your internal purpose along with an inspiring vision and the right habits will allow you to feel fulfilled and at peace.

Think about the difference between passive income and earned income. When income is passive it just happens, you do not need to do anything right now but you have to set up certain automatic processes to make the passive income keep coming and you have to maintain it or pay someone to maintain those automatic processes and now you have it flowing to you without having to do anything!

High Energy Observation: People always think that to achieve more, you must be doing more. But that's not always the case. In most scenarios, less is more. Write down what you no longer need to do so you can eliminate what is holding you back.

WILL POWER IS AN EXCUSE

While I was on my own high energy weight loss journey people would watch me eat salad and say, Joe, you have so much willpower! I wish I had that much willpower.

I laugh because willpower is really an excuse. It's made up. You do not need willpower to eat a salad if you have been eating salad for 2 years everyday and you LOVE salad because it's your new habit.

You do not need willpower to change to decide that you will be focused on foods that are nutritious instead of delicious. You do not need willpower to maintain your new habits, what you need is accountability.

Once you have awareness, and you put the right strategy in place you find that creating the right habits is not a matter of will but a matter of must.

When you transform what you SHOULD do to what you MUST do, you no longer use your will. You are now using something deeper inside you. You become obsessed with creating that habit.

People that are not aware they might WANT something to change in their life but they have something else that is CONFLICTING that they WANT more than what they want to change.

For example you might want to lose weight but what you want MORE than that is to feel good right now by eating a pizza. You try to use willpower to try to stop yourself but you cave.

You give up and say you do not have enough willpower and you even find evidence that willpower is stronger in the morning and you are a night owl so you are doomed to be a midnight pizza eater.

Once you have a commitment to a new external purpose, "To be healthy" you can stay tethered to your internal purpose and be with your new habits. "I love a nutritious salad," and "I do not eat bread because my purpose is to be healthy."

Suddenly eating pizza becomes irrelevant and you are focused on your new habits instead of making willpower excuses.

"Easier said than done," says the voice in our head. "I can't help myself, I'm just exhausted and need to feel good by eating my comfort food"

They are all habits of thought that we are not aware of. The source of the problem. It's not will power, its habits of thought. Realize this will not change overnight, you need to keep at it and you need accountability.

High Energy Observation: Make a list of things you know you need to do and yet are not doing and identify why you feel you must take those actions. Write down the aspects that you will love with the new habit you want to create. If you do not look forward to doing something, you will not want to do it long term. Willpower cannot be relied on long term.

MASTERY COMES FROM REPETITION

If you want to become GREAT at something you need to do it over and over.

When was the last time you did something for the first time?

Then you do it again and again and before you know it, you are a master.

I remember the first time I sat down to write a book. I was terrible at it. I told my coach, I CAN'T DO IT. She said, "Joe, just write everyday and before you know it you will become a master at writing everyday."

The writing did not need to be great, but the act of writing made me great at writing.

Now I can knock out several thousand words in a day and feel really good about the impact I can make on the people in my life by communicating with them about how they can take their life to the next level.

The more you do something, the better you will get at doing that thing.

Greatness does not come as a TALENT but it's a skill and skills are built with repetition. I remember the first time I drove a car, I was fascinated by everything in the car.

After doing it for 20 years, I do not even pay attention to everything I am doing.

I just get in the car and drive. Everything else just happens automatically. Someone on the road gets into my lane and my body moves my car out of the way but quickly makes sure that when I did that I didn't get into any trouble on the second lane.

How did I do that?

It just happened by repetition.

You do it enough times you become really great at it. My friend wants to know how I parallel park so well in Brooklyn.

I asked him how many times he parked the car that way growing up, he said never because he had a driveway to park in.

I said, personally I parked this way over 10,000 times so I can do it with mastery.

It's magical almost because it seems so seamless.

But the magic is really in the repetition.

Growing up I always felt bad that I was bad at basketball but I loved playing the game.

Now looking back, I realized that I did not practice enough. I actually did not practice at all. I judged myself for not being great, thinking I just did not have the talent.

138

I was wrong. It's skill not talent and for skill I needed repetition.

I just wanted to be great without repetition because I did not know that the key was repetition.

What skills do you want to be great at without repetition? What habits do you wish you had right now?

Remember that anything you do over and over again becomes a habit so be careful about what you think about and what you say with repetition because it will become your new reality.

High Energy Observation: What talents do you see that other people have, that you want to have as well? Write down the skills you want to master and commit to taking consistent action with someone to hold you accountable. Want to become a great cook? Take a cooking class and commit to cooking 10 meals a month. Skills are developed overtime with practice.

GREATNESS IS THE SUM OF MANY THINGS HAPPENING AUTOMATICALLY

When you look at the world you see everything happening.

The birds are flying, the trees are standing there, the people are living life.

The sun is shining and the moon is glowing.

You literally do not have to do anything.

You can sit and observe this greatness. It's kind of magical to see how everything just happens on its own.

Personally I am in awe of seeing the effort that goes into creating an automatic process that generates great results.

For example, you start a business and it starts to work.

At the beginning there is lots of chaos with you needing lots of energy constantly to keep things working.

You do not see the greatness in the business because it's a day to day hassle.

Then you wake up one day and decide that all the things that can be repeated need optimized systems and processes.

You create rules, systems, checklists, processes and before you know it, people are just taking action and the business is running like a well oiled machine.

You no longer need to be involved.

When you look at the world you see everything happening.

The birds are flying, the trees are standing there, the people are living life. The sun is shining and the moon is glowing.

You literally do not have to do anything. You can sit and observe this greatness.

It's kind of magical to see how everything just happens on its own.

Personally I am in awe of seeing the effort that goes into creating an automatic process that generates great results.

For example, you start a business and it starts to work. At the beginning there is lots of chaos with you needing lots of energy constantly to keep things working.

You do not see the greatness in the business because it's a day to day hassle.

Then you wake up one day and decide that all the things that can be repeated need optimized systems and processes.

You create rules, systems, checklists, processes and before you know it, people are just taking action and the business is running like a well oiled machine.

You no longer need to be involved.

High Energy Observation: Make a list of systems that are in place in your life that you can be grateful for. Then make a list of systems that you would like to optimize or create to have things in your life be more seamless. Observe those lists and see what comes to you.

CHAPTER EIGHT: ASSOCIATION

ARE THE PEOPLE IN YOUR LIFE SUPPORTING YOU?

Think about the people in your life right now.

Would you say that they are supporting you to live your purpose or are they stopping you from being the best version of yourself?

Family, Friends, Workmates, are they in your life by circumstance or did you attract them, find them and nurture those people?

Chances are that you have many people that have entered your life based on a particular circumstance and you just kept them in your life by default.

Some of those people you love and get energy from and some take the life out of you.

Can you picture that person who is very difficult to be around and you feel like the room just gets a bit darker when they enter?

If you hang around people that complain, that blame, that gossip or have other low vibration habits, you will mirror those people and be on their wavelength.

You are the average of the 5 people you spend the most time with.

The more time you spend with people the more time you are marinating in whatever habits they have that soon may become your habits.

That is why you want to find people who are your champions and cheerleaders that support you when they see your purpose.

The opinions of other people are none of your business but how much time you spend with people who bring you down must be something that you bring to your awareness.

I am not saying to cut toxic people from your life, instead limit your exposure to people who lack awareness.

You can learn a great deal by having limited exposure to people who are driven by their ego and do not know better.

It's a great reminder to get centered and stay centered and focus on our primary purpose. To be accountable you need the right people who will inspire you.

Find those people and cherish them because they will assist you with your purpose.

High Energy Observation: Make a list of people who are your support system and make a list of people you need to spend less time with because they are not supporting your goals. The more time you spend with people who inspire you and support you, the more growth you will experience.

WHO IS THE SMARTEST PERSON IN THE ROOM?

I used to always think I was the smartest person in every room.

I would constantly judge the people that I was with but really I was judging myself.

Being the smartest person in the room you have two options, change the room or change the way you determine what smartest is. If you believe you are always right or you are always the smartest, that belief is a lack of awareness.

The smartest, most intelligent person in the room finds a way to learn from everyone and they do not think they are the smartest in the room, they ask questions instead of shaming and judging other people for not being as clever.

If you think everyone else is an idiot, you might be seeing them through your ego. Instead of competing with the people around you, view them as an ally to support you on your mission.

You no longer need to think that you are the smartest, as that doesn't really matter. When I stop trying to see if I am better, smarter, faster etc, I can start seeing people for who they are.

People crave to be seen.

The best way to get people to support your purpose is to be there for them.

Create a space for the people in your life and watch what happens.

When we stop judging ourselves, it's easier not to judge other people.

Start being selective about the people you allow in your life but make sure that you have the right criteria.

Do not allow your EGO to create the criteria because that will limit your potential massively. I used to want to be in a room just with CEO's that are the leaders of leaders.

When I got into the room with the top CEO's I realized that was the wrong room for me to spend all my time in. Instead I needed to find a room that was not only driven by my EGO to see if I can get there but a room that will nourish my soul.

Having a good mix of people in my life is important to me. If you look at nature you will see diversity.

That is what I want to create for myself. The more diverse the people you spend time with the more open minded and less judgemental you will be.

Do not be the smartest person in the room, be intelligent and create the right rooms for yourself.

High Energy Observation: What type of mentors or coaches do you need to bring into your life in order for you to level up. Are you a big fish in a small pond or are you being inspired and motivated by people who are further ahead? If you want to get hungry, hang around people that are hungrier than you and you will build up an appetite.

WHY WE NEED OTHER PEOPLE

You might think that people just create problems in your life. Relationships can often be very difficult.

The same thing that attracts you to someone will challenge you to the greatest depths.

When we are emotionally attracted to someone, there is something about them that we see can heal us from a wound or from pain.

That is why we unconsciously desire their presence in our life.

That same healing power also has the power to hurt us much more and agitate the emotional wound we have.

We need that agitation to become aware of the source of our hurt. Hurt people, hurt other people.

The best way to heal is to go through the hurt, not run away from it.

Other people will support us, mentor us, teach us lessons we cannot learn on our own.

The right person will say something to you that you heard a million times but the way they said it made it stick.

I had a friend who asked me "Why do you believe that you deserve to suffer?"

I let that question fester because my initial reaction was.

I DON'T BELIEVE THAT.

Anytime you have a conviction about something, a stubborn thought, an opinion that if challenged will almost anger you, it's a sign that your EGO is in play.

Over time I realized that I was allowing certain people in my life with no boundaries because something inside me made me feel guilty about those relationships.

Once I became aware, a brick was lifted from my shoulder and I was free of that burden. I was able to create boundaries with those relationships that helped limit the negative exposure I was getting.

Ask yourself the following question.

What type of people do you need to add to your life?

High Energy Observation: Is your EGO preventing you from having positive and powerful relationships? Ask yourself which relationships in your life need to change. Who do you want to attract into your life?

HOW TO LEVERAGE YOUR ASSOCIATIONS

When you have a relationship you can add value to that relationship by creating space for the person.

You can also leverage your association with people by having them support your purpose.

I want to help 1000 hungry entrepreneurs go from Frustration to Mojovation.

When I meet you, I tell you my vision and you think to yourself, how can I get Joe in front of people who are hungry.

That might help me get another speaking engagement, it might help me get my books out to more people or it might get me featured on a podcast.

If you do not communicate to your relationships how they can assist you, they will not automatically know what to do to serve you.

You might be thinking that, "People that really care about me, would ask me or would already know how to help me." Wrong.

That is the EGO not wanting to get rejected or wanting to feel special. Let go of worrying about having people support you. Let people in your life help you get to the next level.

The whole notion of being SELF MADE is really the EGO manifesting itself to show how great and important it is.

No one is self made.

You get help from people when you least expect it, when you take that leap of faith with someone and it works out.

Leverage your association with people by communicating to them how they can be of service and by sharing your purpose with the right people.

Another way to leverage your association is to get introductions to people that are like them. When creating a Facebook ad, you must select an audience first.

You can upload a list of clients and create something called a "Lookalike audience."

This is very powerful because the technology will go out and find people that have the same characteristics and buying patterns of your clients that you uploaded and you will get more clients.

When you find the right people, usually the people they associate with are often like them too.

So spend time with your friends, friends and watch what happens.

Do you have the attitude of: "I am a giver and I never take." instead create a win-win relationship with people and let them give you.

People get so much more from giving to you than from taking from you.

Let people support you!

High Energy Observation: Do your relationships know how they can help you? Write down the ways that your top relationships can help you and set up meetings with them to educate them about how they can support you with your external purpose.

PEOPLE ARE LIKE MIRRORS

Spending time with people is like spending time with a mirror.

We are programmed to mirror and reflect back what we see.

We are great imitators to the degree that people often look like their dogs.

When people live together they end up looking like each other.

You end up mirroring what people say, what they think and even what they feel.

So you want to make sure that you surround yourself with people who say things that are empowering to you.

People who are full of gratitude and positivity.

Most people are living in fear and they will not be able to be around you if you are a positive, happy and joyful being.

They will try to get you to mirror them instead of allowing your joy to fill them up.

I personally have been told by some people to wipe my smile off my face, it's making them uncomfortable. Instead of wiping my smile away, I find other people to smile with.

Instead of being full of fear, full of shame and full of sadness because misery loves company, be full of light.

Remember that success leaves clues and if you want to have accountability you must find people who hold themselves accountable and are willing to hold you to a higher standard.

People who will not sit complaining about things that they cannot control but have an empowering outlook on life.

One that inspires you to keep growing.

If you live with someone who keeps bringing you down, ask yourself why you are living with them.

Why do you keep allowing this person to kick you off your horse?

You will find that when you are around people who are anxious that you will become anxious just by being around them.

So breathe deep and get centered.

High Energy Observation: Look at yourself in the mirror and ask yourself what you see. Do you feel uncomfortable? Observe yourself and ask yourself, do I look happy? Do I like what I see? Now look at the people in your life and do the same thing. If you do not like the people in your life, they will not like you either.

CHAPTER NINE: APPRECIATION

CAN YOU BE GRATEFUL FOR THE LITTLE THINGS?

It's the little things that make life so great.

We often reserve our gratitude for the BIG moments. I appreciate it when I see a miracle.

YOU ARE A MIRACLE!

That flower is a Miracle.

Remember that everything you see is temporary and when you have that in mind, you will come to appreciate the little things in life.

The wind in your face, the rustle of the leaves, the smell of fresh cut grass or how your own skin feels when you touch it.

You have 5 senses and those are constantly feeding you information.

When you discover your inner purpose and you live it, it becomes easier to notice the little things in life.

We start to see the smile on the face of the people we love, we see the twinkle in their eye that we always missed.

When you are not present, you miss the greatest gifts that we consider small, the ones that pass in front of us all the time.

When we stop to seek, we find that what we are seeking for, is right in front of us. We just have to reach out and take it.

156

Joy, Freedom, Power and the ability for you to feel alive is right there for the taking you just need to get in touch with your consciousness and get centered.

If you cannot feel grateful for the little things this is a sign that you are in your EGO.

Anytime you are stuck in entitlement, lack of appreciation or even contempt you are not vibrating at a high level.

When you are JOY, Gratitude, Peace, are you free and you have the ability to create and connect your inside purpose with your outside purpose.

The ability to stay centered is a skill we must all practice and being grateful for the little things helps us develop this skill.

Make a list of little things that you have been taking for granted.

Like the subway, traveling on airplanes, a napkin or toilet paper, soap, forks and knives.

What helps you have a better life right now?

Running, drinking water? Something delicious that you eat?

People in your life that you love?

Make a list of the small things you want to start being grateful for and look at that list often.

High Energy Observation: Write down a list of small things you are grateful for. Observe that list and allow the blessings to enter your life. The more you focus on what you want, the more of that you will attract into your life.

WHY IS APPRECIATION SO POWERFUL?

When you appreciate you are focused on something outside of you.

You are looking out and seeing, hearing, feeling, experiencing something and you are observing that thing.

Even if it's a thought or a memory that you appreciate, it's not who you are. It's something you appreciate. The mere act of appreciation is observation and it centers you.

You feel good that something in your life happened or that you are with someone that you love.

That feeling that warms your heart is often the fuel we need to get past painful moments, appreciation gives us the fuel we need to not get burned out when we do not get the results we want in areas of our life.

When you appreciate constantly, you are filling up your reserves of positive energy in your body, mind and soul and one who has a full cup can bless others.

The one who fills their cup up to the level of overflow will be able to fill the cups of others too.

Do you want to be a source of blessings and inspiration for the people in your life?

Do you want to inspire yourself and be motivated?

Clarity creates motivation and gratitudes helps you get clear on what is most important, what you appreciate and what you value.

What you value matters, because we are focused so much on what we do not value and that clouds our judgment.

Having a clouded judgment creates fear and fear stops everything.

If you have a strong external purpose and a vision for what you want to create in your life, fear will create chaos and lack of motivation to get you into action.

Appreciation will motivate you to take action and make available emotionally to those around you but also to yourself. Sometimes we need to coach ourselves and just get back up, to be able to see our blindspots on our own by looking in the mirror.

It's hard to see ourselves if the mirror is clouded up.

Appreciation clears up the mirrors so we can see clearly. The harder it is to appreciate, the more you need to do it.

The harder it is to be grateful the more powerful the effect of the gratitude will have on you

High Energy Observation: What is your relationship with gratitude? Do you have a hard time feeling appreciation in your life? Observe your relationship with gratefulness and notice what changes you want to make to include more gratitud into your life. Remember that you cannot be grateful and angry at the same time.

GRATITUDE AS A PRACTICE

Every morning when I open my eyes I am grateful that I am still alive.

I thank Hashem (god) for giving me another day to live. This is not something I decided to do on my own one day.

This is something I was taught by my parents and teachers growing up.

As a practice for each thing that I do, I have been trained to show gratitude and appreciation.

Bless each time I eat, each time I drink, each time I go to the bathroom.

This reminds me to stay in gratitude constantly. Unfortunately growing up it just was a chore for me.

I just did it because I was supposed to do it and so it was routine and I forgot I was doing it.

During my journey to create more consciousness in my life, I realized that I had all these amazing systems and processes for staying centered in my life already.

All I needed to do is be more present during them and connect with the unlimited source of energy.

You may want to create your own gratitude practice via journaling, meditation or even having a gratitude accountability buddy that you share the things you are grateful for each day.

Creating habits in your life that add positive energy, focus and joy to your life is the key to living a great life.

When you make gratitude into a daily practice you will start living your life with more awareness and get triggered less often.

Be grateful for everything that you are, for everything that you have, for all those that you are with, all the time.

I am grateful that you took the time to read this book and I am grateful if you reach out to me and let me know that you enjoyed it and got value from it.

High Energy Observation: What type of gratitude habits do you want to install into your daily routine? What do you think about when you wake up in the morning? What do you think about before you go to sleep? How can you create more gratitude in your life?

PUTTING IT ALL TOGETHER

Now that you have awareness, strategy and a system for accountability you will be able to determine what you want to do with your life.

You no longer need to live a life based on someone else's will or based on your habits that were developed based on someone else's EGO.

Your own EGO is a reflection of the EGOs of the people who you were influenced by.

Now that you have this knowledge it's time to put this into practice.

The first step is making sure you understand your level of awareness about who you really are.

Once you see how incredible your ability of observation is and that you are not your EGO, you start to have AWE at the incredible potential you have.

That awe will make you inspect your agreements to see which ones you have and why you have been living the life you have been living till now.

The second step is to create a strategy by reviewing your skills and resources that you have available to do you. What you want your vision to be for your life and understanding your schedule and your priorities.

The final step is accountability to stay in gratitude, to understand your habits and automate your life by leveraging habits, optimizing who is in your life and being in appreciation of the wonderful blessings we have each day.

When you put it all together you get two things:

1. An internal purpose that is to be aware and stay centered.

2. An external purpose that you choose based on your values and what brings you joy and fulfillment.

Remember that the level of awareness that created the problems in your life is not the same level of awareness that can get you out of those problems.

What got you here will not get you there, you need to transform and level up.

Are you ready to take your life to the next level and be with your high energy purpose?

High Energy Observation: Awareness, Strategy and Accountability. Put them all together and you're going to get your high energy purpose. Take a few minutes to document what purpose means to you and what your vision is for your internal purpose and your external purpose.

ENJOYING LIFE AND LIVING ON PURPOSE

Living life on purpose is actually much simpler than it sounds.

People tend to overcomplicate purpose as this massive thing that must be super inspirational and make everyone go WOW.

No, that's not what Purpose is.

When you see a rockstar on stage giving their all, that's someone living their purpose.

When you see a spiritual leader pouring their heart out to their students, that's Purpose.

When you see a mother being with her kids, fully focused, playing with them, that's Purpose.

Purpose is enjoying what you are doing and doing it enthusiastically.

The more enthusiasm you have, the more connected you are.

If you cannot feel enthusiasm for something that you MUST do, at least accept that you must do it and do not be resentful that you are doing it.

You can enjoy the things that you MUST do even if you do not want to be doing them by letting go of the expectation that you SHOULD NOT BE DOING IT.

166

When we stop blaming other people and just take responsibility for the results we want in our lives we are able to live on purpose and be more present.

Instead of alway trying to do what you love.

Change that around.

Love what you do and love how you do what you do.

If you work at the DMV and people are coming in disgruntled, instead of being disturbed yourself because you do not want to work there and instead you would rather be working as a princess in Disney.

Be magical with the job you are in right now. Make the DMV your own disneyland.

If you are the CEO of a company and you wish you didn't have to do that, instead of wishing things were better, wish that you were better and more aware.

When you focus on what you have in front of you, you can enjoy life.

You can do the little things with more focus, more quality and more enthusiasm which leads to you attracting the things you have in your vision for the future you want to create.

You can only attract a new possibility if you start living it now, it's here already.

Start feeling the feelings that you will feel when you get to your results, this way you not only attract the results but you always enjoy the journey!

Remember this: You are exactly where you need to be right now.

Everything that happened in your life was given to you as a blessing to help other people and to make the future better for yourself and for everyone you care about.

You are enough.

You are worthy of love.

When you stop doing and start being, you are connected to everything.

You were meant to read this book so you can become more aware.

Now share it with others that can benefit from it's concepts

High Energy Observation: What concepts from this book are you prepared to share with other people in your life? What were your key takeaways from this book? Take a moment and write your thoughts down and share them with me.

Email me anytime joe@joeapfelbaum.com

Thank you for being in my life :)

Joe Apfelbaum - Author

ABOUT THE AUTHOR

Want to learn more about Joe? Follow Joe on LinkedIn
www.linkedin.com/in/joeapfelbaum reach out and let Joe
know that you read this book.

Need a speaker for your next event? Joe Apfelbaum is
available for speaking engagements, he is a member of the
NSA (National Speakers Association) and speaks regularly for
entrepreneurs, CEOs, sales directors, and marketing
professionals.

Both for in-person events and virtual events, Joe is
passionate, enthusiastic, and extremely engaging.

Joe has trained over 10,000 business owners on behalf of
Google as a certified Google trainer and has experience
working with as little as 10 people to as many as 5000 at
larger conferences.

Joe Apfelbaum has written several books including his most
recent book High Energy Purpose, How to Be All in on Your
Life and Live Your Truth. The book is about awareness and
how to find your internal and external purpose.

Want to improve your business relationships and
understanding of professional business networking, read
High Energy Networking. Joe breaks down how to leverage
your relationships to get high qualified referrals and new
business.

You can find Joe Apfelbaum's books by searching his name on Amazon or by visiting www.joeapfelbaum.com

Joe is also featured on dozens of podcasts every year and he is a great guest. If you know of a podcast that might benefit from his expertise in business, sales, marketing, or networking, please connect with Joe at joe@joeapfelbaum.com

Do you own a business and want some support with your digital marketing? Check out the digital marketing agency Ajax Union at www.ajaxunion.com - The right marketing strategy will save you a decade and the marketing experts at Ajax Union build smart marketing funnels for companies that want to get an ROI from digital marketing. You can also get Joe's book on Marketing at www.ajaxunion.com/book "High Energy Marketing" will show you everything you need to know about growing your business online.

Need more qualified conversations with potential clients? Learn how to leverage LinkedIn with the Evyrgreen Networking System. Find out more at www.evyrgreen.com You can also get Joe's book on business networking "High Energy Networking" at www.highenergynetworking.com

Made in the USA
Middletown, DE
28 October 2022

13679194R00099